THE HALF-HOUR ALLOTMENT

ROYAL HORTICULTURAL SOCIETY

THE HALF-HOUR ALLOTMENT

TIMELY TIPS FOR THE MOST PRODUCTIVE PLOT EVER

LIA LEENDERTZ

F

FRANCES LINCOLN LIMITED
PUBLISHERS

Frances Lincoln Limited
74–77 White Lion Street
London N1 9PF
www.franceslincoln.com

The Royal Horticultural Society

The Half-Hour Allotment
Design copyright © Frances Lincoln Limited 2015
Text copyright © The Royal Horticultural Society 2015
Photographic copyright © information is listed on page 205

First Frances Lincoln edition 2006

This revised edition 2015

A catalogue record for this book is available from the British Library.

978-0-7112-3681-3

9 8 7 6 5 4 3 2 1

Printed in China

CONTENTS

THE HALF-HOUR PRINCIPLE

Introduction

Everyone wants an allotment these days, and quite right too. Not only is having an allotment a fantastic way to get exercise and fresh air, but it means that you can have complete control of the food that comes into your home. Food scares are a constant concern and the idea of seeing your food through from plot to plate appeals to many people.

We know that food tastes best when fresh, and that supermarket produce is most likely picked a good few days before it reaches us. We may also be aware that flying our beans over from Kenya or apples from South Africa does not help the environment. Some of us realize that the varieties that supermarkets encourage farmers to grow are chosen more often for their ability to withstand the extreme conditions of packing and transporting procedures than they are for taste, and we want to be reminded what real tomatoes and strawberries taste like. Allotments seem a perfect solution to all these worries. The only food miles involved are as often as not those travelled on the back of a bicycle.

But often things go wrong. You may know the story: you get your plot and set about it with gusto. After a few weekends of exhaustion and backache friends start leaving messages wondering what has happened to you, and it suddenly occurs to you that you have been neglecting a few things around the house – and so you miss a week, and then another. By the time you get back to your plot the perennial weeds have crept back, a fresh crop of annual weeds has sprouted, and the areas you had cleared are starting to look much as they did when you started. The rot sets in, and your prized plot soon becomes a source of worry and guilt. Sooner or later a letter from the allotment committee arrives, asking you to maintain your plot to a higher standard or consider giving it up. You bow to the inevitable.

Despite the fact that allotments have never been so popular and many have long waiting lists, a large number of newly adopted plots are abandoned within the year. This is disheartening for allotment committees, but is arguably worse for the poor would-be allotmenteer, left with nothing but a sense of failure and a trapped nerve.

Opposite A well-kept allotment provides healthy exercise as well as the freshest fruit and vegetables you could hope for.

THE HALF-HOUR PRINCIPLE

The half-hour allotment principle outlined in this book was dreamt up by Will Sibley, a nurseryman and allotment holder. Despite the fact that he is constantly on the go, his plot is well ordered and perfectly manicured, and meets a good proportion of his family's fruit and vegetable needs. He has worked out a way to maintain this vision of productivity on half an hour's work a day, with weekends off. The aim of this book is to tap into this system and show you how to do the same.

Will saw that most new allotmenteers take as their role models those plot holders who spend half their lives on their plot. What they fail to see is that for these people their allotment is a way of life. Those of us who cannot put in the same amount of time should certainly not feel inferior. The reality is that when they arrive each day they stand around and have a chat with a neighbour, then stroll around the plot scratching their chins for a bit, before considering their day's tasks. Hours are wasted.

Will Sibley would not call himself a keen gardener so much as a keen eater. He came up with his system because he likes eating good, fresh food, but he didn't want to give up half his life and all his leisure time in order to get it. His experience as a nurseryman gave him the knowledge to do the right things at the right times, and to work with the soil and the seasons. So he set himself parameters, and devised a system that would work for him, and others: people who do not have time to potter, but who like to eat delicious, fresh vegetables.

He thought that there should be a basic minimum return for his investment. The rules went as follows: he would work on the allotment for a maximum of two and a half hours a week, and the allotment would provide a salad and some other green vegetable for his family every day of the year. You may appreciate just how fantastically welcome a plateful of something fresh is in the depths of winter.

So how do you put the system into practice? First and foremost the half-hour principle is about persistence. The best way to keep on top of all the many jobs is to be there regularly. You will need to spend two and a half hours every week at your plot, but this time is really best divided into five half-hour visits, one on each weekday, or into two hour-and-a-quarter visits over two days. Most people can just about manage

ABOVE Sweet and tender: home-grown crops like baby carrots can be captured at their peak and eaten at their freshest.

half an hour of digging. Regular, daily visits also keep you wonderfully in touch with your plot – and a constant presence will help you spot when things need watering, when pests are attacking and the moment when crops are ripe.

Secondly, it is about organization. Ideally you should spend a few minutes at the end of each visit planning your next, but if that is too far a stretch, make a quick tour of the allotment when you first arrive, plan your work in your mind and then get straight down to it. Even better is to break your half hour down into ten-minute chunks – you might measure out 1 sq m (11 sq ft) of soil that needs digging over, sow a small row of carrots and then hoe the weeds under your gooseberry bushes. It doesn't

matter that there is still 29 sq m (312 sq ft) of soil to dig, that you haven't sown your lettuces and that weeds are springing up under your apple tree and loganberries: you'll be back tomorrow, and the next day. This way of thinking will become second nature.

Another rule is to grow what you need, rather than suffering the tyranny of gluts and famine. You may be impressed in your first year when fellow allotment holders start handing out carrier bags full of spinach and courgettes, but you will soon come to realize that almost no one wants courgettes at the height of summer. There is no point in growing 3m (10ft) of French beans that all mature at the same time, sending you into a preserving frenzy, when

Take the principle home

Of course it is possible to grow vegetables not in an allotment but in your own garden. If you have the space you can apply the half-hour principle there. You are far more likely to pop out and do a few minutes here and there in the morning and then again when you first get home from work, and so you are much more likely to keep on top of jobs.such as weeding, watering, and sowing at the right times. In this way, you are likely to be able to reduce the time that you need to spend caring for it: you will have a ten-minute allotment. The equivalent of a quarter plot – about 60 sq m (650 sq ft) – should give ample space to provide plenty of fresh fruit and veg for yourself and your family; you could probably do very well with even less.

ABOVE Plan to grow a range of different crops that will mature in succession, not all at once. This will avoid those annoying gluts that can be dispiriting, especially for a beginner.

you can grow 1m (39in) and have exactly what you need, fresh.

Closely related is careful consideration of the types of vegetables you grow. The idea is that you grow the more expensive, luxury items, and the ones that really benefit from being eaten freshly picked. So you may not grow enough onions and maincrop potatoes to store away and keep you going through the winter, but you will have all the asparagus, raspberries, properly 'new' potatoes and fresh, crispy salad leaves you can eat, plus a year-round supply of sweet, tiny carrots no thicker than your little finger. Will calls it 'dinner-party food'; it is the sort of thing that you would enjoy serving to your guests.

The final tenet is to do everything to make life easier for yourself. There is an allotment tradition of making do, recycling and, above all, keeping costs down. But if you are the sort of person who is happy to spend money on labour-saving devices at home, why shouldn't you do so on the allotment? There is no need to grow eighty times the number of seedlings you need, when you can reach for a catalogue and order the dozen or so that you need to feed your family, already beautifully grown and ready to plant. True, such purchases could be called an unnecessary expense, but if they make your life much easier, and if that makes you less likely to throw in the towel, they're well worth it.

The point of this book is to give you the tools to manage your plot in the minimum amount of time with the least amount of effort. Once you have put in your daily half hour, the rest of your time is your own for chatting, sunbathing, barbecuing or just sniffing the flowers.

Be realistic

If your aim is to grow everything your family will want to eat for the entire year, the half-hour system is not the system for you. We are not trying to achieve Good Life-style self-sufficiency here. Although there will be times of the year when your half-hour plot will supply your entire fruit and vegetable needs, achieving this is not really the point and you are often likely to find yourself supplementing your grown produce with bought. There is no need to feel bad about this – your aim should be to add the luxury of premium-quality fruit and vegetables to your meals, not to supply the everyday, humdrum basics as well.

TAKING ON
A PLOT

Setting up your plot well, right at the beginning, can make a huge difference to its long-term success. This chapter aims to show you how to get hold of a plot and make sure that it is the best of all of those available. It will also give you some guidelines on how to start planning your plot once you have it, and what features to include. If you put some time and thought into getting the basics right, it will improve the ease with which you can manage it and make you less likely to abandon it in the long run.

GETTING HOLD OF THE RIGHT PLOT

If you do not have a suitable plot in your own garden that you can use for vegetables, you will need to get hold of a plot some other way. The most popular way is to rent an allotment on a municipal site; there are also increasing numbers of privately owned allotment sites that you can rent. You may also be able to take over part of the garden of a friend or neighbour who finds their garden too much to cope with. Elderly people, in particular, are often only too pleased to have someone do the heavy garden work they can no longer manage, and may be more than happy with a supply of freshly grown fruit and vegetables as 'rent'.

If you have an option over the type and position of the plot you take on, keep the following in mind.

- **Convenience** Consider how near a plot is to your home. You are much more likely to be able to keep visiting an allotment regularly if you can walk to it within a fairly short time.
- **Water** Find out where the nearest water is. If you are able to use a hosepipe, well and good, but if not, carrying cans of water any distance could become a major job, especially if you are small-framed or at all frail.
- **Access** Even if you are usually able to walk to your plot, having the possibility of driving a car to it allows you to move tools and equipment easily when necessary, and to nip and pick some fresh greens and new potatoes when you have people arriving for dinner in ten minutes. If you can get a vehicle right by the plot (if it is on a large allotment site, for example) it will be very useful when it comes to

having organic matter such as manure delivered. If you can have it deposited straight on to the plot you can just cover it and use it as you need it, avoiding back-breaking hours or even days moving it barrowload by barrowload across bumpy pathways.

- **Shade** Check out how much sun your plot is likely to get each day. Although a little shade is always welcome, it is often better to be able to control it by erecting a shade tunnel or a shelter on a sunny plot, rather than having it forced upon you on a permanent basis. If the plot slopes to the north, the soil will take longer to warm up in spring and lose warmth faster in autumn. Large trees can create dense areas of shade that you will struggle with, and their roots are likely to remove nutrients and water from the surrounding soil, making some areas no-go zones for vegetables.
- **Weeds** Obviously the amount of weeds that cover an unused plot will make a huge difference to how soon you can get

it under control and producing for you. It makes sense to look for somewhere that does not have too many serious weeds, such as brambles, on it. The best scenario is a plot covered in grass, which, although a pain, will be relatively easy to control. You will find details of ways to deal with weeds in Chapter 5.

- **Slopes** Avoid a dramatically sloping plot; it will take hours of back-breaking work to terrace it to make it more manageable. Even a plot that has already been terraced is a pain to get around, especially with heavy equipment and wheelbarrows. Sloping plots are also likely to have drainage problems (dry top, soggy bottom) that will make every planting a complicated decision requiring extra research. Plots at the bottom of a larger slope may also have extra problems with frost, which drains downhill. This can particularly affect your ability to grow some tree fruits that blossom early in the year. A gentle slope to the south, near the top of the hill, is the only good slope.

OPPOSITE A open, sunny plot will give much better results than one that has to put up with a lot of shade. RIGHT Making room for a compost heap is always worthwhile. It will provide valuable organic matter for the soil when it is ready.

HOW MUCH SPACE DO YOU REALLY NEED?

One of the most important factors in managing your plot in half an hour a day is to be realistic about the amount of space you take on, right from the start. It is easy to get carried away when you first get the opportunity to have an allotment – it feels very exciting and liberating suddenly to have all that space at your disposal. But the sheer size of a large plot can soon become daunting.

When you first start out the largest plot you should go for is about 70 sq m (750 sq ft); in fact a plot half this size will probably be sufficient. This makes for a truly manageable area that you will easily be able to get under control; it will be a pleasure to look after and will provide a good selection of veg. It will also give you a chance to learn how to care for and control a vegetable plot without feeling as if you've suddenly gone into large-scale farming.

ALTERNATIVES TO TAKING ON A REDUCED PLOT

You may have no option available but to take on a larger plot than you feel you can cope with. In this case, concentrate first on putting part of it 'on hold'. To go about this you will need to clear the area of weeds, and there are a couple of ways of doing this. One is to use a herbicide such as glyphosate to spray off the weeds on the area that you are not going to use, and the other is to dig out the weeds by hand. You then keep subsequent weeds down by excluding light with a mulch or by strimming or mowing. While herbicides are quick and relatively simple, for many people the second method is preferable, as the whole dream of having an allotment is tied up with the idea of growing organically and attaining a really pure product that has not been adulterated. You may not feel comfortable starting off on your new eco-adventure by using a big

dose of weedkiller. For more information on dealing with weeds, see pages 116–123.

SHARING A PLOT

If you have friends who are also interested in allotment gardening, consider the benefits of a communal approach. There are two ways of sharing your plot. First, you could share a large plot with a friend, half and half. This has the benefit of giving each of you a manageable area and complete autonomy over the crops, layout and approach on your own little patch.

The second way is to both work the same plot. This can be a great way to garden. Although you will need patience and diplomacy when trying to decide exactly what to grow where, you will each bring different skills to the plot, and each be able to put in different amounts of work at different times. You will get the most out of sharing with someone who is at a different stage of life to you. You may be young and fit and full of energy, but perhaps you work full time and can only put in your hours at the weekends. In that case, sharing with a retired person who can pop in daily

to keep on top of the day-to-day tasks such as weeding and watering, but who can't manage the more physical tasks, is perfect.

One of the greatest benefits in sharing is that you have someone to look after the plot during holiday times. These often fall over the warm summer months when vegetables (and weeds) most need your attention, and an overgrown allotment plot full of marrows instead of courgettes, and stringy old beans instead of fresh young ones, is not great to come home to. Having someone to eat the produce as it ripens – so encouraging the production of new leaves and fruits for you to eat on your return – is just as important as having someone to water and weed. You may dislike the idea of having to share your crops, but it is likely that there will always be more than enough to go around, especially if you plan ahead.

PLANNING THE LAYOUT

There are various ways of dividing up a plot. Some people go for a scorched earth policy and make the whole plot into one large bare field. This makes a plot very flexible, as you can really plant anything anywhere, but it doesn't look great. Moving around the plot after wet weather can also be tricky and you will need lots of planks of wood to walk on to avoid compressing the soil and damaging its structure.

The opposite extreme is to divide the plot up into small beds, with paths running in between. The beds could be square ones that can be reached from all sides, or you could make a series of ten or fifteen long beds that run the width of the plot, with paths in between. Doing this would prevent you from ever having to step directly on to the soil. It makes the plot very navigable, no matter what the weather, and ensures that the soil is always in good condition. However, putting so many beds in is a lot of work, they cut down on the space you have available for planting, and they make the space fairly inflexible.

Leaving aside any extra space you may want for a cut flower garden, children's garden, seating area or wild area, consider dividing the majority of your plot into two unequal parts, along its width. Put over roughly a third to permanent plantings, such as soft fruit, fruit trees, asparagus beds and rhubarb plants. The rest is for annual vegetables. It is a good idea to divide this main vegetable area roughly into four. This will enable you to carry out a growing system known as rotation, which ensures you do not grow the same crop, or type of crop, in the same place over subsequent years; this helps to avoid pest and disease problems and also helps to prevent depleting the soil of particular nutrients. You will find more information on the practice of rotation in chapter 6, but you need to think about how you will incorporate rotation into your plot when you start planning. It is easier to adhere to a crop rotation plan if your plot is divided up into individual beds.

Take the long way

Consider dividing the area for annual vegetables into four long, thin beds. Some crops particularly suit this kind of layout.
- Potatoes need to be grown in trenches and then earthed up, and it is simpler to dig one long trench than several smaller ones;
- Beans need a support to grow up and it is easiest to create one large structure in a line than several smaller ones;
- Anything that needs to be covered in fleece or netting, such as brassicas, will be easiest to grow in a long, thin bed, for the simple reason that such fabrics are usually sold in long, metre-wide strips. Growing such plants in blocks can lead to frustrating time spent in complicated stitchings together.

Once you have made these decisions, the next thing to do is to plan everything out. There is no harm, and plenty of fun to be had, in doing this properly, using grid paper and tracing paper. First draw up a plan of your plot as accurately as you can, marking in any existing paths and structures. Then use your tracing paper to draw up several different options. The process of drawing out the various possibilities will free you up to look at your plot afresh and allow you to decide on the best, most practical design.

If your plot is on a municipal site and you are allowed to have a shed, or indeed want one, site it away from any main paths, particularly any that are regularly used by cars. This will make it less attractive to vandals, who always go for the easiest, most accessible sheds first. Placing a shed, along with any other shelter and seating, further back on the plot can make

BELOW Wooden boards make a cheap, easily laid pathway for getting around your plot.
OPPOSITE Paving slabs provide a more costly but longer-lasting path option. They can be laid directly on to the soil with minimal preparation.

it a nice, relatively private spot from which to sit back and admire your handiwork.

A compost heap needs to be carefully sited too. It should be somewhere near the centre of the plot, otherwise you will find yourself constantly walking from one end to the other to fill it. However, it is usually best to site a compost heap away from your main seating area. If you compost correctly, a heap should not have any unpleasant smell, but sometimes they just do and it is far more pleasant not to have to sit near it.

PUTTING IN PATHS

Putting in permanent paths early on is a good investment. They will provide a clean, mud-free way of moving around your plot, and will prevent you from always walking on the soil and so compacting it.

Before you start, think about the various options. The most common type of path is grass. You are likely to be clearing your plot from areas that have been taken over by grass, and so making a grass path may simply involve leaving a strip untouched when you are digging over the rest. Although such grass paths are cheap and simple to create when starting out, there are some drawbacks. Much of the grass on allotments is of the tough, weedy variety known as couch grass, which spreads by creeping into uncolonized areas, such as your newly dug-out beds. You will need to continually pull out the little blades of grass that pop up near the edges of your beds, as well as the running roots that have taken them there. One way around this is to create paths from scratch with new turf. They will still need mowing and edging but should not grow quite as vigorously and will not be such a bad source of weed infestation. All grass paths harbour slugs and snails,

RIGHT Edging gravelled areas with stone, wood or metal will keep things tidy and prevent gravel from spilling out across the growing area. Underlay gravel or any surface aggregate with a weed-suppressing membrane.
OPPOSITE Well-placed paths not only allow you to move around the allotment without trudging through mud, they also help to avoid soil compaction.

and that can become a real problem for your plants: slugs will hide in grass and under the edges of paths during the day, and then crawl out at night to chomp any tasty emerging young shoots, such as seedlings that you have just planted out.

You may conclude that you will make life easier for yourself in the long run if you create paths from hard landscaping materials, such as patio paving stones or gravel. Although this means more of an investment of time, energy and money when starting out, it will cut down on both maintenance and potential problems. If you are using patio pavers, you will simply need to level the path area and place them on top of the earth; there is no need to use mortar and a bed of sand on the allotment as you would were you laying a patio or path at home. If the pavers are adjacent to an area of grass that will need to be regularly mown or strimmed, dig the area out so that they sink down to the same level as the grass. This will mean that you will be able to run a mower straight over the edges without damage.

If you choose to go for a loose path material such as gravel, bark chippings, clinker or even cockle shells, it is a good idea to lay a weed-suppressing fabric underneath (this is sometimes known as landscape fabric). This should be porous, so that it lets moisture through (you don't want rainwater forming big puddles on your paths, as it would if you used thick plastic or a similar material), but it should be thick enough to exclude all light, so that weed seeds beneath it do not germinate, or cannot thrive if they do. You can spread your path materials direct on to this membrane, although you might also consider edging the path with strips of wood, in order to keep the contents neat and tidy. An added benefit of sharp materials such as shells and gravel is that they create inhospitable environments for slugs and snails, which cannot travel over them comfortably, and so such paths are less likely to harbour anything that will crawl out and cause havoc when your back is turned.

RAISED BEDS

Another option to consider right at the start is raised beds. The effectiveness of these will depend on your soil type and on what you want to grow. You create a raised bed by framing a bed with planks or strips of wood, usually held in place with wedges of wood driven into the soil, and then filling it with topsoil and manure, compost or whatever other well-rotted bulky organic matter you have available. Among the benefits is the fact that raised beds warm up faster in spring than the rest of the soil does, and this can mean that seeds germinate earlier and therefore you can get crops sooner than you would otherwise. They are also particularly useful if you want to control the soil type in order to grow crops that do not do well in your normal soil. My own plot is on a very heavy clay soil and it is hard to grow crops that require good drainage. A raised

area filled with topsoil, with plenty of grit mixed in for extra drainage, provides the perfect environment for herbs such as thyme, oregano and even basil, which would quickly perish if planted direct into the thick clay. By filling a raised bed with an acidic, ericaceous soil you could also grow plants such as blueberries, which thrive in such conditions, in an area with a predominantly alkaline soil, in which blueberries would perish. Where raised beds become less useful is on well-drained soils, where they can have a tendency to dry out far more quickly than surrounding soil, causing problems for the plants within them and creating extra work for you.

Although it is on this sort of small scale that raised beds may be most practical for most people, it is possible to put your whole plot over to them. You would benefit from this particularly if you have a troublesome, heavy soil, or if you have mobility or back problems, as raised beds bring the area

OPPOSITE As well as keeping things tidy, high-edged raised beds allow for the addition of plenty of soil additives, such as manure, without risk of overspill. ABOVE Tall raised beds can be a real boon to gardeners with mobility or back problems.

to be tended slightly closer to you. If you really struggle to bend, ask your allotment secretary about the possibility of creating more permanent brick or wood structures to bring the soil up to waist height. Some allotment societies are particularly open to this as a way of keeping older or less able people on their plots; there may be some raised beds set aside strictly for their use, or practical help may be available instead.

Simple wooden edges will define your beds. Although they will not have any effect on the make up of the soil within them, they are good for keeping back weeds with running root systems such as couch grass, which can gradually creep on to beds. They are another tool for making the plot easier to manage.

Essential tools

Before you get started, set yourself up with some tools. You will need as basics

- spade
- fork
- rake
- hoe
- hand fork
- trowel

Some extras to consider include

- **Hand cultivator** – a three-pronged instrument that you drag through the soil and can use for a great number of jobs, including grubbing up weeds and creating a fine tilth in which to direct sow seeds
- **Border spade** – if you are of small build, or find digging hard going, a border spade is much more petite than a normal spade and can make lighter work of a hefty digging job
- **Shears** – these will be useful to keep your grass paths and edges neat
- **Watering can** – see also Chapter 7 page 138.

Seating and shelter

While the half-hour ideal is all about getting in and out quickly, taking no prisoners, there is no harm in considering a few luxuries to make life more pleasant. The inclusion of a sheltered area with seating on your allotment can provide a place for rest and reflection and make it a very pleasant spot to spend some time on a summer evening. If you have no other access to garden space and your vegetable plot is to be your substitute garden, it is definitely worth putting in a little effort to make your rest times more comfortable.

Even if you are really pressed for time, you might still be able to fit in a few minutes of rest between each ten-minute bout, or a little sunbathe once you've finished. For those who get easily worn out, or who suffer from aches and pains, some seating and a little shelter can be a godsend. It is also handy to have a place to sit your allotment neighbour down and give them a biscuit and cup of tea from your flask, while you lightly grill them for all their hard-earned gardening knowledge.

SEATING IDEAS

Somewhere to sit may mean nothing more elaborate than a lump of wood or the step of your shed, but you could go further and create a bench from scraps you find lying around the site. A couple of neat stacks of bricks and a plank of wood would be perfect. If you are not the DIY type, a fold-out camping chair makes perfect allotment seating, as it is light and easy to move about, but folds up flat for shed storage.

Check the rules

Always check allotment regulations before building or assembling any kind of permanent structure. Different sites have different rules, and you do not want to go to all the trouble of making a perfect sheltered seating area only to be told to dismantle it next time you arrive.

SHADE AND SHELTER

It may seem a bit of an effort to create shade and shelter on your plot, but on a baking hot summer's day or during a fit of spring showers, being able to duck under cover can make the difference between finishing what you've started and abandoning all for home and a dry pair of socks.

You may have a tree on your plot that is large enough to give you cover, and if it is of a suitable shape you could even suspend a tarpaulin between the branches to create a dry seating area. Pieces of wood hammered together to create a small porch, with a piece of roll-out bamboo screen tacked to the top, castaway-style, look great. A piece of clear plastic secured over the top would make it waterproof. You can also use a shelter as a practical extension of your

allotment. A rough framework of well-secured bamboo canes can be used to support sweet peas, peas or beans, which will create their own shade just when it is most needed. Builders' pallets are particularly useful for this kind of thing. They could be stacked end on end and fastened together to make walls, or simply be laid on the floor of your shelter to create a mud-free island. Old patio slabs or even just planks of wood could be put to work as flooring.

HOME COMFORTS

As well as all the practical reasons for creating seating and shelter, there are

ABOVE A sheltered corner provides the ideal spot to sit down and take a break from your labours.
OVERLEAF Seating does not have to be expensive or elaborate. An old bench that is past its prime still allows you to recharge your batteries, perhaps alongside an allotment neighbour.

good psychological ones too. The more structures and permanent features you can put into place on your allotment, the more manageable it becomes. Once your feature is in place, there is less space available to be taken over by weeds, and when everything is mud and dead grass in the depths of winter, you at least have something to prevent that blasted-heath look.

Setting up a shed

Not every plot has the luxury of a shed, but it can make so much difference to the efficient running and organization of an allotment. It all depends on the way you arrange your shed, and the things that you keep in it. Purely in terms of time management, a well-stocked and well-organized shed makes sense. If you have to take everything you might need with you every time you go, you can use up your entire half hour just in preparation. A shed will reduce the amount of time it takes you to get out of the house and up to the allotment. If you just chuck your tools in your shed at the end of a session that's fine; it is serving its basic purpose well – but you could certainly make better use of it with a little bit of planning and thought.

SHED SECURITY

When you first get started, think about shed security. Allotment sites are empty and lonely places at night, and as such are irresistible to thieves and vandals. Most theft on allotments is opportunistic. It is caused by bored kids with nothing better to do and only rarely will there be a properly organized attempt on your tools. Thieves are after things with good resale value, such as new, shiny, high-quality tools and machinery, so if you have anything fitting this description, don't keep it there. Carry any posh bits of kit home with you at the end of a session. Buy a set of old, cheap and battered-looking spades and rakes from a car boot sale and leave those in the shed. If you really must have good ones, and can't carry them back and forth for some reason, at least get them a bit mucky by smearing mud on the shiny bits and on the handles.

ABOVE A shed allows you to keep tools and equipment on site instead of having to carry them backwards and forwards from home.
OPPOSITE Even a shed that needs a few running repairs is a valuable asset for the allotment holder,

TO LOCK OR NOT

You can go one of two ways when it comes to securing the shed. The obvious way is to make sure that the door of your shed fits well, with good, solid hinges and fixings, and to lock it up with a good, chunky padlock. However, a padlock can act as a bit of a magnet for unwanted attention, making it look as if you have something worth protecting, and many allotment shed doors are not solid enough to withstand said attention for long. A determined allotment thief has all the time in the world and knows he is unlikely to be disturbed in the middle of the night. The alternative may sound a little scary, but it seems to work just as well. It is to not lock your shed at all. Making the shed look as if it is not worth breaking into is at least as good a deterrent as making it look as if it will be hard to break into. For that really ramshackle look, prop the door closed with a couple of bits of wood.

When setting up your shed, consider alternatives to glass windows, as these are particularly attractive to vandals. Put in a piece of thick translucent plastic instead, or just cover the window hole over with a wooden board. If you inherit a shed, spend a little time smartening up the roof to make it weatherproof, as this protects both shed contents and structure from damp. Once this is done, perhaps with new roofing felt in place, install gutters and a rain barrel, which not only prevent pools of water from forming around the shed after a heavy downpour but also provide a handy store of water on your plot, avoiding the necessity for you to collect water every time you need it.

An extension to the downpipe that can be swung between a series of barrels will allow you to collect water all winter long, even after your first barrel is full.

AGAINST THE RULES

Some strange allotment sites and societies have rules against erecting sheds. This always seems a real shame, and not only for practical reasons. Sheds bring so much character – a shedless site can look quite barren and bleak. It also leaves you with a problem regarding tool storage.

Where sheds are allowed, it is common to have to apply for written permission from the site management first. You are usually not permitted to set sheds or any other structures on solid foundations such as concrete pads or brickwork.

Often there is a height restriction that effectively excludes sheds, and you can get

around this by investing in a long box with a lid that you can cover in roofing felt, to keep it waterproof. Buy one long enough to fit your tools, as well as other bits and pieces; this can also double as a seat.

As a temporary measure, wrapping your tools in a piece of old carpet keeps them dry and hides them from potential burglars while making your plot look like it contains nothing worth stealing.

ABOVE As your range of gardening equipment increases you will be glad of a safe, secure place to store it away.
OVERLEAF Sheds help to add a touch of quirky character to an allotment site.

Shed contents

In addition to the basic tools that you will keep in your shed, you might also consider including any of the following as permanent residents:

- a garden line to help you plant or sow in straight lines
- plastic bags for harvesting
- secateurs
- a bucket for collecting weed roots
- a pair of old shoes, an old coat, an old sun hat
- sun cream
- a folding camping chair
- some labels and a pen
- a hammer, screwdriver, screws and tin of nails for running shed repairs
- a plank of wood for standing on and working off
- a tape measure

DECIDING WHAT TO GROW

When you have first cleared your plot, the space available to you will seem endless, especially if you are used to the confines of a small town garden or courtyard. Even a half or a quarter allotment will stretch away from you, making you feel that you will never fill it up. But you will be surprised at how wrong this impression is. Plants take up space. You are likely to make plans for growing a huge variety of crops, and then find, come late spring, that you have filled up all the space you have available and have to give away all your beautiful tomato plants to neighbours. If you have a reduced plot, say a half or a quarter of a traditional plot, space will be at a particular premium and in order to be able to manage it more easily you will need to make every plant work hard.

CHOOSING YOUR CROPS

You may already have a good idea of the crops you want to grow before you even set foot on your plot, but before making the final decisions, you need to look at the realities of growing each crop, and whether crops are good or bad value in terms of the space and attention they will demand.

OPPOSITE Runner beans require supports, but their huge cropping potential makes the extra work involved well worthwhile.
RIGHT Radishes are among the quickest and easiest crops for a beginner to try.

The good and the bad

There are a number of reasons why a plant can be good or bad value, in the context of the half-hour plot.

Bad-value plants
- Take up a lot of space over a long amount of time before cropping
- Do not produce high yields
- Are prey to particularly virulent pests and diseases and so demand a lot of effort to make them produce good-quality crops
- Are cheap and easily accessible from supermarkets, and so not worth the effort of growing

Good-value plants
- Germinate easily
- Mature quickly
- Have few problems from pests and diseases
- Take up little space
- Benefit from being eaten really fresh

There are relatively few crops where deciding on their value is straightforward, as most have both good and bad factors. You will also have to weigh these up with your love for the final product.

Take, for example, purple-sprouting broccoli. This has major drawbacks. The plant is big and needs to be in the ground for a long period of time – plants planted out in late spring need almost 1 sq m (11 sq ft) each, and they will not crop until the following late winter or early spring, and then only for a few weeks. On the other hand, the crop is extremely tasty, expensive to buy and difficult to find in the shops. To decide whether to grow it, you must weigh up the pros and cons, depending on the space you have available.

Some crops, however, are very easy to define as good value. Mixed salad leaves and lettuce must be the ultimate good-value crop. They are at their crisp and juicy best when freshly harvested, rather than bought in sweaty supermarket packets; they germinate and mature incredibly quickly, and take up little space; and they taste great. They can also be squeezed, both physically and temporally, between other crops, either in small rows between slow-growing crops or filling a space where something else is due to be planted later.

Dwarf French beans are high scorers too, because they are expensive to buy, each plant is compact and hugely productive, and once they are in the ground they involve almost no care.

ALTERNATIVE CROPS

In several cases it is worth considering alternatives to poor-value plants. Peas are best avoided, partly because they are martyrs to pests such as pea moth and pea and bean weevil, and partly because they are cheap to buy. On the other hand, mange tout is a gourmet ingredient that can be hard to find in the shops and is always expensive when you do. The plants are highly productive and do not involve the same level of pest and disease heartache that you suffer when growing peas. Peas, therefore, are low value and mange tout high value.

Onions are pretty easy to grow and do not take up too much space, but they are so cheap to buy that growing them

DECIDING WHAT TO GROW

is a false economy. Spring onions and shallots especially are as easy to grow but are far more interesting crops and have more unusual flavours and applications. Shallots are also expensive and less easy to find in the shops.

One crop over which there can be little argument is maincrop potatoes. These are so cheap to buy in the shops that it seems pointless to grow them on an allotment. New potatoes, on the other hand, have a distinct edge over their maincrop relatives: they are high value mainly because they really must be eaten fresh out of the ground. This is the crop that deteriorates the most once harvested and, no matter how hard they try, supermarkets and greengrocers will never be able to match the freshness and taste that you get when you pull a handful of new potatoes out of

the ground, take them home and boil them that evening.

GROW WHAT YOU LOVE

While it might be helpful to bear in mind which plants are the best value, don't let it be the only criterion you employ. The most important thing is to choose and grow plants that you love to eat. If you hate mange tout and love purple-sprouting broccoli, then grow purple-sprouting broccoli you must. This should be the golden rule: grow vegetables that you love to eat. A surprising proportion of

allotmenteers grow crops because they are given seed, or they think they are proper 'allotment plants', and then end up giving them all away to their neighbours.

SEED OR PLANT?

There is something life-affirming about nurturing a plant from seed; the first sign of a shoot pushing its way through the earth is a truly heart-warming moment. However, there are problems with growing vegetables from seed.

Indoor seed sowing is an incredible amount of fuss. Most new allotmenteers, trying to fit a little vegetable growing around a busy lifestyle and with little space at their disposal, will not have invested in a greenhouse. If this is the case for you, you will end up with every windowsill and table in your house groaning with seedlings (seed packets usually contain large amounts of seed, so you always end up with too many plants). These seedlings will soon need pricking out, a massive job involving hours of your time, huge numbers of pots and large volumes of compost. Without a greenhouse, you will spend most of mid- to late spring avidly watching the weather forecast and hoicking your more tender seedlings such as tomatoes and pumpkins in and out, while running the risk that one day you will forget and lose the lot.

Some hardier crops can be sown in a nursery bed on the allotment and then put into place at a later date. Although this is not quite as tricky as windowsill propagation, it has its drawbacks. You will still end up with many more plants than you need, and the root disturbance when you transplant the young plants can seriously set them back. A nursery bed also takes up valuable space.

Plug plants

The answer is wonderfully straightforward: get someone else to grow your seedlings for you. Seed companies have only relatively recently caught on to the potential of making vegetable plug plants available to amateur gardeners, but this is a development we should embrace wholeheartedly. The companies that do this are experts. They grow plants perfectly and supply them in fabulous condition. Some companies will even supply plants at the moment at which they should be planted out – the plants just turn up on your doorstep at the correct moment and all you need to do is nip up to the allotment and pop them into the ground.

BELOW Plug plants can be easier and often more economical than raising your own plants from seed.

Get set...

Onions and shallots are slightly different to most plants, as they can be obtained as sets – small, immature bulbs – rather than plug plants. It is always worth choosing sets over seed if you are trying to grow vegetables in a limited amount of time and space. You will have less choice of cultivar, but set-grown crops need be in the ground for a far shorter period of time than seed-grown ones, and planting sets is much less fuss than sowing and planting out seed.

ABOVE Onions sets are quick to plant and should be spaced around 10cm (4in) apart for the best results.

Specialist vegetable plug plant suppliers have a good range of cultivars that you can obtain by mail order, but when you are starting off, you will probably be able to buy all the plug plants you need from a garden centre.

Plug plants are not always the answer, but there are a few situations in which they definitely come out on top. Use them whenever you need only a few plants in order to get a good crop – courgettes, for example, a few plants of which produce enough fruits to feed a whole street, let alone your family and friends. Use plug plants wherever you would otherwise need heat or shelter to produce frost-tender seedlings such as tomatoes in the early part of the year. And choose them above seed sowing whenever plants need to be spaced well apart, as with brassicas.

Plug plants are more expensive than plants grown from seed, but this is one point where the needs of the half-hour gardener are at odds with traditional allotment values. There are occasions, such as this, when spending a little frees up so much time and spares you so much bother that it is worth it.

SEED SOWING

There is still a place for seed sowing on a half-hour allotment, and that is when they can be sown direct into the ground where they are to mature. For many crops, buying plug plants would be ridiculously expensive because of the number of plants you would need, and the trouble involved in planting each out individually would far outweigh that of sowing seed. As a general rule, the half-hour allotmenteer should only buy seed that can be direct sown. Sowing in this way is far removed from the palaver and inconvenience of sowing in pots or trays indoors (see page 188) or even sowing into a nursery bed.

A good guide is to direct sow those crops that grow closer than 15cm (6in) to

each other. These include carrots, spring onions, beetroot, parsnip and mixed leaf lettuces. All of these are best sown in drills, left to germinate and then thinned to the correct spacing. In some cases, as with close-sown carrots, the thinnings themselves are edible; raw carrot thinnings make a lovely, sweet, crunchy addition to salads. This is far better for the plants than being sown in nursery beds and then yanked up and placed in their final positions. It means that those that you leave behind will have an intact and undisturbed root system. For some plants that are grown slightly further apart, such as French and broad beans, the relatively large seeds are easy to space sow individually.

Close contact

Although thinning out can seem like extra work, it gives you the chance to get down on the ground near your seedlings, and provides a good opportunity to weed them thoroughly. Weeding can be a little tricky with direct-sown seeds, as weed seedlings and vegetable seedlings are likely to germinate at the same time and look very similar, at least at first. One of the best ways around this is to sow in lines, rather than to scatter the seed across a larger area. A definite line of seedlings will germinate and you will know that they are probably your vegetables, not weeds, and you can then weed all around them. As you become more experienced, you will be able to differentiate between weed seedlings and your vegetable seedlings, but when you are first starting out, leave everything in the line until the seedlings start to look different from each other.

Another problem with seed sowing is the constant, preying presence of dreaded slugs and snails. These exist on every allotment in huge numbers and love eating tender, juicy seedlings above all else. Unhindered, they can be devastating, wiping out rows of seedlings in a single night. You will need to protect any directly sown seedlings from them. For information on dealing with pests, see chapter 8.

PERENNIAL PLANTS

When it comes to evaluating perennial vegetable and fruit plants, things get a little complicated. You might think that they are low-value plants because they take up so much space all year round and have relatively short cropping seasons. But although they are great space-hoggers, their permanence is part of their attractiveness for the gardener with limited time. Once perennial plants are established, they need only the minimum

amount of care to keep on producing crop after crop. You need to maintain them, true, but you will never need to think about sowing them or buying in plants again until the time comes to replace them, and that can be many years later. On a small plot you may feel you do not have space for perennial plants, but if you do decide to give an area of your plot to them, it will be almost self-maintaining.

Luxury crops

Another reason for growing perennial plants is that almost all of them produce really luxurious crops. An allotment without raspberries would be a sad place. Although they are big plants, they are incredibly easy to grow and utterly delicious. The same goes for all the other soft fruit: loganberries, strawberries, gooseberries, rhubarb, redcurrants and blackcurrants all make delicious, vitamin-packed additions to a family's menu and all are very easy to care for. Asparagus takes up lots of space, but it is so delicious and so expensive to buy that it would seem a real shame to miss it out.

If space is really limited, there are ways that you can squeeze these crops in. There

are some, such as rhubarb and asparagus, that cannot be trained or encouraged to grow in any way other than the obvious. But both soft and tree fruit plants can be trained so that they take up only a little space on the ground.

The right rootstock

Not all allotment societies allow fruit trees, mainly because of concerns that they will grow too large and shade neighbouring plots, so you need to check the rules before you start buying and planting. Fruit trees can become very large, and they can be a problem if gardeners do not know what they are looking for when they buy them and then let them grow freely. However, they are also easily controlled if you choose the right plant and prune it correctly.

With fruit trees for confined areas, the most important factor is the rootstock. All fruit trees that you will find in garden centres or from specialist suppliers are grafted on to a rootstock, rather than grown from their own roots. Rootstocks control the vigour of the plant, so whereas an apple cultivar grown on an MM111 rootstock might grow up to 10m (33ft) in height, the same grafted on to an

OPPOSITE Trained trees allow fruit to be grown even in a restricted space.
TOP LEFT Plums can be grown on dwarfing rootstocks such as Pixy to keep them compact.
TOP RIGHT Juicy pears are a real treat, and when grown as espaliers or cordons they take up little space.

M27 rootstock might reach only 2m (7ft). The largest rootstock you should go for when choosing apples is an M9, which will reach 3m (10ft) even if left to grow freely. With pears, look for Quince C rootstock, and with plums and gages, go for Pixy or St Julien A.

Getting into training

In addition to choosing the correct rootstock, you can keep fruit trees small through training. You might think that this would severely reduce the amount of fruit that they produce, but in fact, the bends and corners that are required to make the plant grow in a particular shape force the sap to move more slowly through the plant, and this leads to more tough, fruiting growth being formed, at the expense of the lush, sappy green growth that the tree would put on if allowed to grow freely. Top-fruit trees, such as apples, cherries, peaches, pears and plums, can be trained as espaliers, cordons or fans, all of which keep the growth on a strictly vertical plane. This means that they take up hardly any precious allotment space, and can even be grown along the boundaries.

A really neat way to grow apples is as stepovers. These comprise a single horizontal branch, growing on a leg; they are therefore very low-growing and can be literally stepped over. They make wonderful edging plants for beds and boundaries. You can either buy trees as young plants and train them yourself, using a system of wires, or you can buy plants that are several years old and have already been trained into various shapes. This is an expensive way of going about it, but very convenient, and will give you an instant effect. As well as being productive, trained fruit trees look beautiful and can be a real feature on your plot.

Soft fruit

Soft fruit, such as blackcurrants and raspberries, can also be trained to make it fit into your limited space more snugly. You should certainly grow plants such as loganberries, blackberries and raspberries along a fence or a system of wires, so that they take up only a limited amount of space on a very strict plane. It is less commonly done, but there is no reason at all why gooseberries should not be grown as cordons, espaliers or fans. In fact, the sharp thorns of the gooseberry often make harvesting extremely tricky when they are grown as bushes, as they usually are, and growing them as espaliers (similar to stepovers but with a series of parallel branches) allows the fruit to hang down below the thorns and be more easily picked.

Both gooseberries and redcurrants do well grown as standards – that is, with the bushy part of the plant atop of a bare upright stem. Again, the fruit can hang down and be more easily picked, and growing them this way also allows plenty of air circulation around the base of the plant, which helps to keep down fungal diseases. It is a great example of the way you can manipulate plants in order to fit more into your plot, while increasing productivity and plant health at the same time.

GROWING THE BEST VARIETIES

OPPOSITE Studying the seed catalogues gives you the
chance to try some slightly less conventional varieties,
such as these pale green courgettes.

One of the main reasons most people bother with this whole allotment
business, rather than simply buying fruit and veg from a supermarket,
is that they think that home-grown food tastes better than commercially
grown food. But the unfortunate truth is that tastier food does not come
automatically with owning an allotment or vegetable patch. It is still
possible to produce bland crops, or get bored because you have grown too
much of one crop and have had to eat it night after night for two months.

GROWING THE RIGHT CULTIVARS

Growers who supply fruit and vegetables
to supermarkets have to concentrate on
producing large and perfect-looking crops
with a long shelf life; they grow cultivars
that are most likely to look good and
produce the highest yields, rather than
choosing those that are the best tasting.

On the half-hour plot, on the other hand,
you are not looking to be self-sufficient but
to supplement your diet with tasty, fresh
and nutritious food, and to amaze your
dinner-party guests with the intensity of
its flavours. You will be able to search out
the tastiest crop varieties; specialist seed
suppliers can advise you. And don't forget
to talk to your allotment neighbours; the
chances are that they have come across
a few unusual favourites, particularly
if they have been at it for a few years.

ABOVE A bunch of tasty beetroot is a genuine success
to share with your neighbours or friends.

They will also be able to tell you what crops grow particularly well on your site, and equally what not to bother with. Learn from their successes and failures, rather than forcing yourself to learn from your own.

FEAST AND FAMINE

Most allotment holders will be familiar with the experience of suddenly having to deal with a glut of certain vegetables. Say you grow a 10m (30ft) row of French beans; they will all reach perfect harvesting stage at the same time. The first few plants will give you perfect beans, just a few inches long and still tender and tasty. After a couple of weeks the beans will be getting tougher and stringier, and by the time you are halfway through the row, you will probably be so fed up of beans that you throw them all on the compost heap.

The technique for growing just enough crops to keep you satisfied is simple. You sow or plant smaller amounts, and in some cases you sow these small amounts successionally, over a period of time, so that separate sowings of the same crop come to the perfect point of ripeness every few weeks, rather than a huge amount being ready at once.

WHAT TO GROW, HOW MUCH TO GROW AND HOW TO GROW IT

The chart on pages 68–87 is designed to help you decide how much you need to sow, or how many plants you need to plant, in order to feed a typical family of four. Amend these figures according to the amount of people you need to feed and, of course,

to suit your own tastes. If you really love a particular crop, and are likely to eat it every day when it is in season, you will need to grow more. There are tips on how best to get a good succession of young, tender vegetables from each crop. In addition, the chart tells you whether the crop is easiest grown from plants purchased at the garden centre or through specialist growers, or if it is simpler to sow it direct.

Not every vegetable is included in this table. It covers only those crops that Will Sibley and I consider good-value for the half-hour plot. The criteria for this vary from crop to crop, but each has at least one of the following attributes:

- it is a gourmet vegetable or fruit that is particularly tasty
- it is hard to track down in the shops or
- expensive to buy
- it takes up little room on the plot, or does not need to be in the ground over a long period of time
- it is particularly easy to grow

The tips outlined for growing each crop are not necessarily the definitive techniques – for many crops there may well be many other methods you could use – but they are the techniques that we consider the most productive for gardeners with small plots and limited time to spend on them.

OPPOSITE TOP Unlike many commercial growers, you will be able to grow strawberries for their flavour, not just for their uniform looks.
OPPOSITE BOTTOM LEFT Growing small amounts, successionally, is the secret to avoiding gluts.
OPPOSITE BOTTOM RIGHT Look for quick-maturing radishes with excellent flavour.

◀ APPLES

Plant only those grafted on to dwarf rootstocks (M9 or M27) and buy these trained as cordons or stepovers so that they stay compact and do not take up too much space.

PLANT OR SEED: Plant

QUANTITY: Three stepovers or cordons

TIPS: Choose a selection of disease-resistant cultivars for a succession of ripening times and to ensure cross-pollination

GENERAL INFO: Plant when trees are dormant in a sunny, sheltered site. Prune in winter, shortening side growths from the main stems to create many fruiting spurs

RECOMMENDED CULTIVARS: 'Pinova' (early autumn ripening), 'Park Farm Pippin' (mid-autumn), 'Red Falstaff' (mid- to late autumn)

LEFT TOP Apple trees trained to be compact will still produce enough fruit for most families.
LEFT BOTTOM 'Pinova' is an exceptional apple which ripens early and also stores well.

ASPARAGUS ▶

Takes up lots of space on an allotment, but too tasty to miss out on. Perennial, so pretty straightforward to maintain once established after two or three years.

PLANT OR SEED: Crowns

QUANTITY: Ten crowns

TIPS: Cut at least every other day from when spears start to emerge

GENERAL INFO: Plant in early spring into very free-draining soil. Plants must be left to grow for two or three years before you start to cut them. From mid-spring for six to eight weeks, harvest spears that are sticking out of the ground by 12–18cm (5–7in), cutting 2.5cm (1in) below soil level to get blanched stems. Enjoys seaweed fertilizer

RECOMMENDED CULTIVARS: Choose all-male cultivars that will not go to seed, such as 'Backlim', 'Gijnlim', 'Jersey Knight'

RIGHT Asparagus spears will need cutting every other day, or every day in hot weather.

◀ AUBERGINE

Very tasty, but will grow only in the sunniest, most sheltered site outdoors. Elsewhere, grow under the protection of a cloche, cold frame, greenhouse or polytunnel. There are several unusual cultivars that you cannot find in the shops.

PLANT OR SEED: Plants

QUANTITY: Three plants of different cultivars to give a variety of shapes and harvest times

TIPS: Regular picking before the fruits are too large encourages more fruits to appear

GENERAL INFO: Plants should arrive around late spring, and they should be planted out then but kept under cloches until early summer. Grow in your sunniest and warmest spot. Put cloches back on as weather cools to ripen the last few

RECOMMENDED CULTIVARS: 'Bonica' and 'Ronde de Valence'

LEFT TOP Aubergines are best grown as young plants under a cloche or cold frame or inside a polytunnel. LEFT BOTTOM Choose three different aubergine cultivars for a longer, more varied harvest.

BROAD BEANS ▶

Delicious when small and a very good early crop.

PLANT OR SEED: Seed

QUANTITY: Two 3m (10ft) rows

TIPS: Best eaten when young and tender, so sow at intervals and pick when small. Autumn sowing produces tougher plants that are less susceptible to attack by blackfly, but the seed may rot over winter in heavy soils

GENERAL INFO: Direct sow seed in autumn or spring 23cm (9in) apart. Pinch out the tips of blackfly-infested plants when the flowers have set, as they attack and breed on the softer parts

RECOMMENDED CULTIVARS: 'Super Aquadulce' (good for overwintering for earliest crops), 'Imperial Green Longpod' (particularly tasty)

RIGHT Autumn-sown broad beans give the earliest crops. Pick the pods when they are young for tender, tasty beans.

◀ DWARF FRENCH BEANS

Dwarf cultivars are incredibly easy to grow, requiring no support and almost no attention but producing lots of beans over a long period.

PLANT OR SEED: Seed

QUANTITY: Two 3m (10ft) rows

TIPS: Sow at intervals during growing season to produce beans from early summer to early autumn. Pick every third day to keep pods young and tender

GENERAL INFO: Direct sow in moisture-retentive soil, as plants respond well to water. Make the first (mid-spring) sowing under cloches as seedlings are tender to frost; remove cloches when danger of frost has passed. The last sowing can be in late summer. Water regularly

RECOMMENDED CULTIVARS: Choose dwarf rather than climbing cultivars, as they are much easier to look after. 'Aquilon' (early and productive), 'Delinell' (large crops), 'Triomph de Farcy Stringless' (old gourmet type with great flavour)

LEFT Pick French beans frequently, when they are young and tender; older pods become stringy and tough.

RUNNER BEANS ▶

A little fussy, as they need support, but will produce tasty beans well into autumn.

PLANT OR SEED: Plant and seed

QUANTITY: One 4m (13ft) row

TIPS: Pick every three days from mid-summer until early autumn

GENERAL INFO: Construct a solid support. Add plenty of organic matter to soil to retain moisture. Buy your first lot as plants and plant out 30cm (12in) apart, in late spring. At the same time sow two seeds between each plant (one may not germinate or may be eaten). This allows a succession of plants without the need to construct a new support for the second sowing. Water well throughout season

RECOMMENDED CULTIVARS: 'Red Rum' (particularly tasty), 'White Lady' (lovely tender pods), 'Scarlet Emperor' (old favourite)

RIGHT The colourful flowers of runner beans mean they are welcome anywhere as a pretty climber, not just in the vegetable plot.

◄ BEETROOT

Very easy to grow, although some people may not want them as they take quite a lot of preparation to get them to the table.

PLANT OR SEED: Seed

QUANTITY: Two 3m (10ft) rows, sown at intervals

TIPS: Easy to grow but can have a tendency to bolt in dry weather, so keep well watered. When harvesting, twist rather than cut the leaves off to minimize bleeding

GENERAL INFO: Direct sow at intervals, with first row in late winter. Thin to 10cm (4in) apart when seedlings are large enough. Repeat with second sowing in early summer. Start picking when golf-ball sized from late spring onwards

RECOMMENDED CULTIVARS: Boltardy' (resistant to bolting), 'Burpees Golden' (yellow flesh), 'Chioggia' (candy-striped), 'Detroit 2 Crimson Globe' (best flavoured, sweet, almost black flesh)

LEFT Start pulling beetroot when they are golf ball size, from late spring until late summer.

BROCCOLI AND CALABRESE ►

Delicious, mature very quickly and have antioxidant properties.

PLANT OR SEED: Plants

QUANTITY: Twenty per planting, three plantings

TIPS: Lots of plants are necessary as each produces a fairly small head

GENERAL INFO: Plant 30–60cm (12–24in) apart in rows; first planting in mid-spring, second in early summer and third in late summer. Final planting will overwinter. Protect from birds, particularly in spring. Likes a warm spot

RECOMMENDED CULTIVARS: Calabrese: 'Belstar' (good flavour), 'Samson' (produces sideshoots once main head is cut)

Sprouting broccoli: 'Early Purple Sprouting, 'Late Purple Sprouting', 'White Eye' (white, early sprouting)

RIGHT Calabrese is exceptionally nutritious and merits three separate plantings in mid-spring, early summer and late summer.

◄ BRUSSELS SPROUTS

Controversial: some people hate them but to others they are delicious. Can be picked over a long period of time.

PLANT OR SEED: Plants

QUANTITY: Twelve plants

TIPS: Brussels sprouts are supposed to get sweeter and have the best taste after they have been subjected to the first frost. Pick as you need them over a long period of time

GENERAL INFO: Plant out in late spring. Normally plants are placed at 1m (39in) intervals, but closer spacing at 38cm (15in) allows them to support each other and prevents wind rock. For best winter crops, keep well watered throughout summer

RECOMMENDED CULTIVARS: 'Cromwell' (early cropping, good flavour), 'Rubine' (unusual red-coloured sprouts)

—

TOP LEFT Set out in late spring, young Brussels sprouts will be well under way by the arrival of summer.
LEFT Sprouts can be harvested over a long period through the winter. Start picking from the bottom of the stems.
BELOW Cold and frosty weather is thought to make sprouts sweeter and improve their flavour.

▲ SPRING CABBAGE

Very tasty and welcome in spring.

PLANT OR SEED: Plants

QUANTITY: Twelve plants

TIPS: Pick and eat as required

GENERAL INFO: Planted in autumn, 30cm (12in) apart, plants should be ready to harvest throughout the following spring

RECOMMENDED CULTIVARS: 'Pixie' (tasty, pointed type), 'Hispi' (good taste, pointed type)

TOP Plant spring cabbages in autumn, setting them around 30cm (12in) apart and firming them well.

◀ WINTER CABBAGE

Easy to grow and tasty.

PLANT OR SEED: Plants

QUANTITY: Ten plants

TIPS: Pick as required through winter

GENERAL INFO: Plant out in early summer into well-manured ground. Can be particularly susceptible to cabbage white butterflies and pigeons: cover with a frame draped in Enviromesh or netting. Harvest from mid-autumn throughout winter

RECOMMENDED CULTIVARS: Savoy varieties are the tastiest: 'January King' (best-flavoured Savoy and very hardy, but not as crinkly-leaved as some), 'Tundra' (the hardiest cabbage and good for cold areas)

LEFT Crinkly-leaved Savoy-type cabbages have a particularly fine flavour and stand throughout the winter.

◀ CARROTS

Easy-to-produce crop for the whole year. Sweet and tasty.

PLANT OR SEED: Seed
QUANTITY: 3m (10ft) rows sown every three weeks during growing season
TIPS: When pencil thick, thin out every other one to eat raw in salads. Eat the rest as required. Late summer sowings can be eaten throughout winter – you may want to sow a couple of rows for this purpose
GENERAL INFO: Direct sow seed thinly in succession with first sowing in late winter and repeat at three-weekly intervals until late summer. Thin plants to 2.5cm (1in) apart and discard thinnings. Give lots of water throughout summer. Harvest small carrots by wiggling the tops until the roots loosen: lifting with a fork will disturb too many plants. If carrots are hard to pull, water ten minutes before harvesting. Protect from carrot fly
RECOMMENDED CULTIVARS: 'Primo' (earliest for first sowing of year), 'Early Nantes' (all year round), 'Nanco' (for late summer sowings to stand into winter), 'Paris Market' (globe type, good on clay soils), 'Flyaway' (carrot fly resistance)

LEFT The ferny foliage of carrots may be attractive, but benefits from covering to exclude carrot fly.

CAULIFLOWER ▶

A good tasty crop, but avoid growing too many.

PLANT OR SEED: Plants
QUANTITY: Six plants
TIPS: Plants produce large heads, so you can quickly get tired of them if you go for too many plants
GENERAL INFO: Like all cabbage family plants, cauliflowers need well-firmed soil when planting. Space plants 60–75cm (24–30in) apart, depending on variety. Plant out in spring for summer harvests and in early summer to harvest throughout the winter from late autumn onwards
RECOMMENDED CULTIVARS: 'All The Year Round' (traditional variety, good for successional sowing) and 'Graffiti' (a striking deep purple variety maturing in autumn)

RIGHT TOP The large, snowy-white heads of cauliflower can be harvested throughout the winter.
RIGHT BOTTOM Set young cauliflower plants out in well-firmed soil in spring and early summer.

◄ CELERIAC

Harder to find in the shops and far more expensive than celery, but easier to grow and with a similar taste. Delicious mashed together with potato.

PLANT OR SEED: Plants
QUANTITY: Eight plants
TIPS: Plants grow huge – up to 1kg (2lb) each – so do not grow too many
GENERAL INFO: Plant out in early summer and harvest from late autumn to the mid spring as required. Likes lots of water through the growing season and hates getting dried out
RECOMMENDED CULTIVARS: 'Monarch'

LEFT Celeriac is well worth growing as it is not readily available in the shops, where it can be expensive.

CHARD ►

Highly productive, has a delicate flavour and is a colourful addition to the kitchen. Use leaf or stalk steamed or stir-fried, or use the young leaves in salads.

PLANT OR SEED: Seed
QUANTITY: Two 3m (10ft) rows
TIPS: Tolerant of most conditions and treatment. Will regrow several times after cutting
GENERAL INFO: Direct sow first row in early spring and second in late summer for continuity of leaves. Thin seedlings to 15cm (6in) apart and start cutting, with scissors, as soon as large enough
RECOMMENDED CULTIVARS: 'Bright Lights' (colourful stems), 'White Silver' (pure white stems and dark green leaves)

RIGHT Chard's rainbow stems add a welcome touch of colour to both plot and plate. Both leaves and stems are edible.

◀ CHICORY

Tasty winter salad crop.

PLANT OR SEED: Seed

QUANTITY: One 3m (10ft) row

TIPS: For the best-quality leaves, grow under cloches in winter

GENERAL INFO: Sow direct into the row in late spring and thin out seedlings to 15cm (6in) apart. Harvest throughout winter as required. To produce blanched chicons you will need to lift and pot up some roots in late autumn or early winter and keep them in a shed or greenhouse at about 10–15°C (50–60°F). Exclude all light from the shoots with black polythene or similar material

RECOMMENDED CULTIVARS: 'Jupiter' (red), 'Palla Rossa' (traditional red), 'Zoom' (Witloof type, good for forcing)

LEFT Plump white chicons are a salad delicacy produced by forcing chicory plants in the dark.

COURGETTES ▶

Tasty, tender, essential summer crop. Delicious griddled on the barbecue or even eaten raw if picked young enough.

PLANT OR SEED: Plants

QUANTITY: Four plants

TIPS: Courgettes are the classic glut plant and each plant will make huge numbers of fruits. For the tastiest crops pick every day when the fruits are just a few inches long, or they will soon turn into marrows

GENERAL INFO: Buy two plants and plant them in late spring. Two weeks later buy two more plants and plant them out. This way not all your plants will ripen at the same time. Give plants lots of space – they will need at least 1 sq m (11 sq ft) each. Plant out after frosts have passed, as they are very tender. Give lots of water throughout the summer

RECOMMENDED CULTIVARS: 'Parthenon' (very early, sets well even in poor weather), 'Gold Rush' (good flavour, yellow fruits, highly productive), 'De Nice a Fruit Rond' (round, pale green fruits), 'Custard White' (white, scalloped edge)

RIGHT Pick courgettes when they are very young. You can even enjoy them raw at this stage – they have a lovely nutty flavour.

◄ GARLIC

Essential part of much modern cooking and easy to grow. Requires drying and storing but does not take up much space.

PLANT OR SEED: Bulbs
QUANTITY: Three bulbs (up to thirty cloves)
TIPS: Harvest all when mature and dry to use through winter
GENERAL INFO: Plant in autumn, at 18cm (7in) spacings. Requires lots of sun and good drainage. Bulbs swell up and split into cloves when they first start growing in spring, and copious watering at this time will encourage the best-quality crops. Harvest midsummer
RECOMMENDED CULTIVARS: 'Thermidrome', 'Solent Wight' (large bulbs, good flavour)

LEFT Garlic is a kitchen essential and easy to grow. Plant cloves 18cm (7in) apart in a sunny spot in autumn.

CURLY KALE ►

Delicious gourmet vegetable for winter steaming. Easy to grow and each plant will crop several times.

PLANT OR SEED: Plants
QUANTITY: Fifteen plants
TIPS: When harvesting, cut out the centres of the plants to eat them as required. They will grow again
GENERAL INFO: Plant out in early summer about 25cm (10in) apart, in well-drained soil. Protect from whitefly. Will put up with extremely low temperatures over winter. Harvest from early autumn through winter
RECOMMENDED CULTIVARS: 'Redbor' (dark red leaves and good flavour), 'Reflex' (green, very hardy)

RIGHT Curly kale is a particularly hardy winter crop. Leaves continually regrow to provide a long harvest period.

◀ LEEKS

Cheap to buy but worth growing for the difference in taste between home-grown crops and commercially grown crops, which are also subject to high levels of chemical sprays.

PLANT OR SEED: Seed or plug plants

QUANTITY: Six 2m (7ft) rows

TIPS: When weeding, draw a hoe between the rows to earth up young plants slightly. Begin to harvest as soon as large enough

GENERAL INFO: Direct sow seed at 8cm (3in) intervals in rows 30cm (12in) apart in late spring. This close spacing makes them tall and slim and encourages self-blanching (the stems stay white and tender rather than turning green). Harvest during winter and into spring from one end of row to the other; do not thin out or blanching effect will be lost. During mid-spring, plug plants can be dropped into small holes made with the handle of your hoe, and watered

RECOMMENDED CULTIVARS: 'Apollo' (vigorous, slim-growing leek), 'Musselburgh' (strong flavour), 'Bulgarian Giant' (particularly good for close spacing)

LEFT Plant leeks close together to produce a self-blanching effect; the white stems will be tastier and more tender.

LETTUCE ▶

Easy to grow and at its best when freshly harvested. Good cut-and-come-again crop.

PLANT OR SEED: Seed

QUANTITY: One 2m (6ft) row sown every four weeks

TIPS: Buy a packet of mixed leaves or several packets of different types and mix them together. Use scissors to cut as much as you need each day, cutting the entire plant at around 5cm (2in) from ground. Do not store but eat immediately. Plants will resprout and can be cut again several times. Always cut the largest plants first

GENERAL INFO: Direct sow every two weeks from early spring to early autumn. Prefers a cooler spot with some shade. Keep well watered but wet the soil rather than the leaves or else the leaves will rot. Harvest as necessary

RECOMMENDED CULTIVARS: Combine as many different types of salad leaves as you can find: cos, little gem, oak leaf, frilly and red lettuces, rocket and mustards

RIGHT Sow lettuce in a cool, lightly shaded spot in summer, as hot conditions can prevent good germination.

◄ LOGANBERRIES AND OTHER HYBRID BERRIES

Hybrid berries are big-cropping plants, with much higher yields than blackberries.

PLANT OR SEED: Plant

QUANTITY: One plant

TIPS: For best-sized fruits, water as the fruit is swelling

GENERAL INFO: Plant in late autumn in the middle of a sturdy, long-term support (two strong stakes with wires strung between). In autumn, cut the fruited stems down to the ground after harvest, and tie in two new shoots horizontally; these will bear next year's fruit

RECOMMENDED CULTIVARS: 'LY59' (loganberry), tayberry, boysenberry

LEFT Hybrid berries such as tayberries are very productive, producing large, tasty fruits.

MANGE TOUT AND SUGAR SNAP PEAS ►

More expensive vegetable to buy than normal garden peas but easier to grow.

PLANT OR SEED: Seed

QUANTITY: One 3m (10ft) double row

TIPS: Start picking as soon as pods are around 3.5cm (1½in) long

GENERAL INFO: In early spring, direct sow into rich, well-manured ground with seeds at 15cm (6in) spacings, then another row of seeds in between but offset by the same spacing. This allows you to push twiggy supports in between for the plants to climb up. Keep soil moist by watering regularly during dry spells

RECOMMENDED CULTIVARS: 'Oregon Sugar Pod' (sweet and crunchy mange tout type), 'Sugar Ann' (snap type)

RIGHT Pick mange tout peas while the pods are still flat, before the peas inside begin to swell.

◄ MELONS

Delicious, although a greenhouse or polytunnel is essential in cool summers.

PLANT OR SEED: Plants or pre-chitted seed (seed is particularly hard to germinate)

QUANTITY: Six plants

TIPS: Not possible to grow a succession in cooler climates where there is only necessary warmth long enough to grow one crop

GENERAL INFO: Plant in early summer. Need lots of water to ripen well. If you cannot use netting to support the fruits, rest fruits on a tile or piece of wood to keep them off the soil. Pick when skins start splitting near the stem and the fruits give off a characteristic aromatic fragrance. Eat as soon as possible after harvest

RECOMMENDED CULTIVARS: 'Sweetheart', 'Outdoor Wonder'

—

LEFT Support ripening melons in nets to prevent the heavy fruits breaking their stems.

ORIENTAL LEAVES ►

Unusual and varied crop that is hard to find and expensive to buy in shops. Particularly useful for stir-fries.

PLANT OR SEED: Seed

QUANTITY: Two 4m (13ft) rows

TIPS: Good cut-and-come-again crop. Cut with scissors as required when plants are young and tender. Not good for summer sowings as they can bolt. Can be grown out of doors through winter or under cloches, and can be cut during this time until leaves get too stalky

GENERAL INFO: Direct sow in late summer. Plants will overwinter well

RECOMMENDED CULTIVARS: Look for seed mixtures of oriental vegetables, or make your own by combining packets of pak choi, Chinese cabbage, mizuna, mustards and green-in-the-snow

—

LEFT Seed packets of mixed varieties of oriental leaves give a quick and easy crop for salads and stir-fries.

◄ PEARS

Grown on dwarfing rootstocks, pears can be kept relatively compact. Only grow those trained as cordons or stepovers, or else they will take up too much space.

PLANT OR SEED: Plants

QUANTITY: Three plants

TIPS: Watering well for the six weeks after flowering will give big, juicy pears. Grow a variety of cultivars to ensure good pollination and a succession of ripening times

GENERAL INFO: Plant when dormant in a warm, sheltered site that is not in a frost pocket. Pears love water, so give as much as possible. Prune in winter to thin out damaged, diseased or overcrowded growth. Pick while still firm when they begin to change colour and ripen indoors for one to three weeks

RECOMMENDED CULTIVARS: 'Williams Bon Chrétien' (early autumn ripening), 'Concorde' (early autumn), 'Doyenne du Comice' (the best tasting pear – ready in mid autumn)

LEFT Keeping the soil moist for six weeks after flowering will help to ensure the juiciest pears.

SWEET AND CHILLI PEPPERS ►

Easy to grow with just a little protection.

PLANT OR SEED: Plants

QUANTITY: Sweet peppers: six plants; chilli peppers: one plant

TIPS: Plants will keep on producing fruits as long as you keep picking. Pinch out the flowers of sweet peppers towards the end of summer, as otherwise the existing fruit will not ripen

GENERAL INFO: Plant in your sunniest, most sheltered spot in late spring under cloches. Remove cloches when weather heats up. Provide lots of water

RECOMMENDED CULTIVARS: Sweet peppers: don't bother with the basic pepper that can be bought in the shops but instead go for more interestingly shaped cultivars such as 'Hamik' (small, orange and sweet) and 'Marconi Rossa' (a deep red, long pepper)

Chilli peppers: 'Cayenetta' (good for first-time growers, tidy habit), 'Hungarian Hot Wax' (good all-rounder, not too hot),'Thai Dragon' (very hot)

RIGHT Chilli peppers are easy to grow. The more you pick the fruits, the more will be produced.

◀ NEW POTATOES

Much more tasty and expensive to buy than maincrop potatoes. At their best when eaten fresh.

PLANT OR SEED: Seed potatoes
QUANTITY: 3kg (7lb) bag
TIPS: Dig and eat as required
GENERAL INFO: Get the potatoes into the ground as early as possible to get an early crop. In warmer regions this will be in early spring, but you may need to cover the ground with fleece. Pre-chit the seed before planting (i.e. keep them in a light, cool but frost-free place from midwinter so that they can sprout). Plant with a few centimetres of soil covering them, 30cm (12in) apart. Earth up by regularly covering the top growth with soil as it appears, to prevent greening of potatoes and to protect from frost. When flowers appear, water well. Ready about seventy days after planting
RECOMMENDED CULTIVARS: 'Anya' (salad potato), 'Home Guard' (brilliant flavour), 'Epicure', 'Swift' (particularly early cultivar)

LEFT Cook and eat new potatoes as soon as possible after harvesting – their flavour will be a revelation.

RASPBERRIES ▶

Tasty and easy to grow.

PLANT OR SEED: Plants (known as canes)
QUANTITY: Twelve plants
TIPS: Autumn raspberries are the simplest to grow and start cropping as early as mid-summer, so do not bother with summer raspberries if space and time are limited
GENERAL INFO: Plant canes in late autumn 38cm (15in) apart into well-prepared soil. Provide good, strong support and tie plants in as they grow. Water as fruits swell. At the beginning of each winter, cut the canes of autumn raspberries down to ground level. Prune summer raspberries in autumn; cut the fruited stems down to the ground, and tie in new shoots to horizontal wires; these will bear next year's fruit
RECOMMENDED CULTIVARS: 'Joan J' (long cropping season), 'Autumn Bliss' (good flavour)

RIGHT Autumn-fruiting raspberries are the type to cultivate if space is limited, as they have a long cropping season.

◀ REDCURRANTS

Very attractive plants when in full fruit. Ripe currants can easily be frozen for later use.

PLANT OR SEED: Plants
QUANTITY: Two plants
TIPS: For best-sized fruits, water when the fruit is swelling
GENERAL INFO: Plant between autumn and early spring. Train plants into a fan shape against a wire frame, rather than as a freestanding bush, as this makes fruit easier to pick and takes up less room. Prune in early spring; cut back new growth at end of each branch by half and remove any overcrowded, damaged or diseased branches
RECOMMENDED CULTIVARS: 'Rovada', 'Red Nose'

LEFT The glistening, translucent fruits of redcurrants are both attractive and good to eat.

RHUBARB ▶

Easy to care for and delicious, as well as being the first fruit of the year.

PLANT OR SEED: Plant
QUANTITY: One plant or 'crown'
TIPS: Stems should always be 'pulled' rather than cut: pull the stems away from the crown using a twisting motion. For the best crops, follow blanching instructions. Do not eat leaves, as they are poisonous
GENERAL INFO: Add well-rotted organic matter to soil before planting from mid-autumn to early spring. Do not remove any stems during the first year. For the earliest and most tender stems, blanch or 'force' by placing a plastic bin with the bottom cut out over the plant in winter before it has started into growth. Fill with straw for extra warmth. Pull the stems as soon as they are more than about 23cm (9in) long. Stop pulling around mid-spring and remove bin to give the plant a chance to recover for the rest of the year. Mulch with well-rotted manure and water well. Unforced plants can be harvested into summer
RECOMMENDED CULTIVARS: 'Champagne' (fine flavour), 'Stockbridge Arrow' (bright red sticks)

RIGHT Rhubarb stems can be made extra tender and succulent by blanching them with special forcing pots or ordinary plastic bins.

◄ SHALLOTS

As easy to grow as onions, but better, sweeter, more interesting flavour. Also more expensive and hard to get hold of in shops.

PLANT OR SEED: Sets (small bulbs)

QUANTITY: Twenty bulbs

TIPS: It is essential to keep weeds down

GENERAL INFO: Plant bulbs 20cm (8in) apart from midwinter to early spring in well-manured ground. Water well in early and mid-spring when just starting into growth. Lift when leaves start to turn yellow and leave to dry in a cool, dry place for about ten days. Store and eat as required

RECOMMENDED CULTIVARS: 'Golden Gourmet' (large bulbs, mild flavour), 'Griselle' (excellent flavour)

LEFT Choose shallots over onions for a more interesting crop. They are harder to find and more expensive to buy in supermarkets.

SPINACH ►

Easy-to-grow, cut-and-come-again crop, which is highly nutritious.

PLANT OR SEED: Seed

QUANTITY: 3m (10ft) rows

TIPS: Make sure that plants never dry out, as this can make them go to seed

GENERAL INFO: Direct sow each row every two months during growing season with the first sowing in early spring. Each plant can be cut, using scissors, several times before it is exhausted. Make last sowing in early autumn and cover with a cloche for cropping throughout winter

RECOMMENDED CULTIVARS: 'Galaxy' (good for baby leaves for salads and larger leaves for cooking), 'Apollo' (mildew-resistant)

LEFT Baby leaves of spinach are ideal for use in salads. The leaves can be cut several times as plants soon regrow.

◄ SPRING GREENS

Very rapid-growing looseleaf cabbage. Tasty and nutritious, and will stand all winter.

PLANT OR SEED: Plants
QUANTITY: Thirty plants
TIPS: Pick as required throughout winter
GENERAL INFO: Each plant does not produce a huge amount, so plant relatively large numbers of plants across plot, 23cm (9in) apart, in mid-summer to eat from early autumn onwards
RECOMMENDED CULTIVARS: 'Greensleeves', 'Excel'

—
RIGHT Spring greens are particularly high in vitamins and other essential nutrients, and can be harvested all through the winter.

SPRING ONIONS ►

Very easy-to-grow ingredient that adds interest to salads.

PLANT OR SEED: Seed
QUANTITY: 2m (7ft) rows
TIPS: Water well in dry conditions
GENERAL INFO: Direct sow each row thinly every four weeks from early spring to early autumn to crop from mid-spring to mid-autumn. Make final sowing of a few rows to grow through winter
RECOMMENDED CULTIVARS: 'White Lisbon' (mild flavour, use for summer and winter), 'Furio' (red onion, mild flavour)

—
LEFT Spring onions are a good-value crop because they are quick to grow. It is always useful to have a bunch to hand in the kitchen to add to cooking.

◀ SQUASH

Takes up a lot of space, but really delicious, especially cut up and roasted. Unusual types are available that you will not find in the shops.

PLANT OR SEED: Plants
QUANTITY: Two plants
TIPS: Cure and store to eat when required
GENERAL INFO: Needs lots of feed and moisture. Dig planting pit and fill with well-rotted manure before covering the top with soil. Plant direct into hole as soon as frosts have passed. Water well throughout season. When mature, cure the fruits by cutting them off the plants, stem attached, and leaving them to dry in the sun for a week or so. Move indoors if wet weather or frost threaten
RECOMMENDED CULTIVARS: 'Uchiki Kuri' and 'Crown Prince' are both tasty and beautiful

RIGHT Winter squashes such as 'Crown Prince' store well and make a delicious and unusual vegetable.

STRAWBERRIES ▶

Particularly worth growing if you can get hold of the older cultivars, which are far tastier than the modern commercial ones.

PLANT OR SEED: Plants
QUANTITY: Ten plants
TIPS: Pick and eat as they mature
GENERAL INFO: Plant out in mid-spring in two rows of five plants. Place straw closely around all the plants to keep the fruits off the mud once they appear. Keep well watered but do not wet the fruits or else they will rot. Pick fruits from the first year. Plants will need replacing after three years
RECOMMENDED CULTIVARS: 'Gariguette' and 'Mara des Bois' (both fairly low yielding but particularly tasty older cultivars)

RIGHT To avoid strawberries rotting, keep the fruits off the soil and avoid wetting them when watering the plants. It is best to harvest and eat them as soon as they are ripe, before any chance of spoiling or damage by pests.

◀ SWEET CORN

A crop that is really at its best when eaten fresh, but it takes up a lot of space for the amount it produces and may not mature well in cooler areas, so it is not for everyone.

PLANT OR SEED: Plants
QUANTITY: Twenty plants
TIPS: Harvest and eat as mature
GENERAL INFO: Needs a sheltered spot and lots of moisture, so work well-rotted organic matter into the soil and water regularly in dry spells. Plant out as soon as frost has passed. For best pollination and crops plant in a 'grid' or 'block' formation with plants 45cm (18in) apart. As soon as the tassels start turning brown, test for ripeness by peeling back skin and bursting a kernel. If the juice is clear it is not yet ripe, if it is milky it is perfect, no juice and it is overripe. Eat soon after harvesting
RECOMMENDED CULTIVARS: Look for 'supersweet' cultivars: 'Mirai Gold', 'Earlibird', 'Swift'

LEFT Sweet corn is picky about its growing conditions, but if you have a sheltered spot and rich soil you can enjoy mouth-wateringly sweet cobs.

TOMATOES ▶

Taste so much better home-grown than bought that they are an allotment essential. Extremely versatile and tasty.

PLANT OR SEED: Plants
QUANTITY: Ten plants
TIPS: Grow as many as ten different cultivars to give a variety of tastes, harvest times and uses. Pick and eat as mature
GENERAL INFO: Need sunny sheltered spot out of strong winds if possible. Buy nice strong plants and once frosts have passed plant out into ground rich in organic matter. Insert strong stake to support plants. Remove side shoots as plants grow and tie in regularly. Give plenty of water, particularly as the flowers are setting. Do not wet the leaves. Grow under cover if possible. Tomatoes grown outdoors are often hit by blight
RECOMMENDED CULTIVARS: Cherry: 'Cherry Belle', 'Sungold', 'Rosella'
Beefsteak and marmande: 'Black Russian', 'Super Marmande', 'Costoluto Fiorentino'
Plum: 'Santonio', 'Roma'

RIGHT Home-grown tomatoes have a far better flavour than most shop-bought ones. Little cherry tomatoes are particularly popular with children.

KEEPING ON TOP OF YOUR PLOT

Everyday maintenance may not be the most fun part of having an allotment, but it is probably the most important. If you can keep on top of the everyday jobs, you will avoid having to spend long weekends catching up with the weeding.

The best way to avoid the feast-and-famine approach to allotment tasks is to try to make the half hour you spend there each day an integral part of your daily routine. Make it as routine as having a shower in the morning or catching the bus home at night, and it will cease to seem like a chore and just become a part of your everyday life. It will become more and more enjoyable as you get the plot more under your control.

THE BEST USE OF YOUR TIME AT THE ALLOTMENT

If you arrive at your plot and then start wandering about, checking out the various jobs that you could do, you can lose so much time. Decide what work you are going to do on your next visit before you leave; this gives you the chance to plan ahead and make sure that you have all the tools that you will need with you.

There are two main approaches to managing your time at the plot, depending on the sort of jobs that need doing and their urgency.

Make it routine

One of the simplest ways of incorporating a half-hour regime into your life is to make it part of a daily commute. Make a decision to leave the house three-quarters of an hour earlier than usual, and you will catch the allotment at a magical, peaceful time and have the site almost entirely to yourself. Call in on your way home from work and you will have an opportunity to relax and de-stress from the problems you have faced in the day. If you work from home, are retired or your plot is near your place of work, do your half hour before you eat your lunch every day.

Achieving large tasks

The first approach is to break down a large job and do it over several half hours. This is probably the approach you will employ during the busy times, and when there are particularly large, urgent or daunting jobs to do. It is important not to be too ambitious about how long such jobs are going to take you. Saying things like 'I will plant out the potatoes in today's half hour' is not realistic. There are several elements to this job, each fairly time-heavy and taxing to the muscles, and by overstretching yourself at the start you will only end up over-running your time and getting worn out, or leaving the job half done and getting dejected.

Instead, dedicate your first half-hour session to roughly digging over the ground where the potatoes are going to go. This may even take two sessions. Use the following session for planting, and one a few weeks later for earthing up when the first growth appears. The job will have taken you three, or maybe even four sessions, but you will not have broken your back doing it, and will have reinforced your pattern of daily visits. Try to start thinking about all larger allotment jobs in

this way. How can they be broken down into several distinct jobs, each amounting to one manageable session?

Breaking down the half hours

The second approach is to break the half hour down into shorter, ten-minute sessions. This can be more useful once things calm down a little as autumn approaches, when you are keeping the allotment ticking over and the jobs to be done are less urgent. At times like these you may think there is little point in keeping up your daily visits, but in fact on any allotment there is always something that needs doing. By tackling a few small jobs each time you will keep your enthusiasm up, and you will be in intimate contact with all areas of your plot so that you know exactly what needs doing next.

PRIORITIZING AND PLANNING

There will be times of the year when the number of jobs that need doing seems overwhelming and you will not know where to start. Just remember that you can't do everything at once, and some things are going to have to be put to the end of the

priority list. Try not to feel guilty about this. There is simply too much to do in some seasons — spring, in particular — for you to be on top of everything. But what should you do first?

Picking and harvesting This job should always be a priority. You should expect it to be pretty time-consuming, and even occasionally to take up the whole half hour, particularly in mid- and late summer. Bear in mind that the whole point of tending an allotment is to have nice things to eat. If you are letting crops go beyond their best because you are so busy weeding and watering, there is really no point to all your hard work. Each day, decide what you want for dinner that evening and as soon as you arrive at your plot, pick just the right amount for that night or the next. If

you do this every day, harvesting should always remain relatively manageable. The only exception to this rule is when you are picking salad leaves in hot weather, when it might be best to wait until the end of your half hour to prevent spoiling.

Sowing and planting Getting things planted or sown at the right time is really important, as you can easily miss your window of opportunity and some things will never catch up if sown too late. But keeping track of what goes in when can be one of the trickiest jobs. A good idea is to set up a card index system at the beginning of the year, when your seeds arrive. Make cards for each week of the year and put each seed packet into the week it needs sowing (you can split seed packets for crops that need to be sown successionally). Using the information in the chart in chapter 4, you could also put in reminders for when you need to buy vegetable plants from the garden centre. Another approach would be simply to set up an allotment calendar at the beginning of the year with all the timings already written on it, and to check it at the beginning of each week.

Watering and weeding The jobs with the next highest priority are those that have most impact on the quality of the crops you are growing. It is not possible to keep your plot weed-free at all times, so draw up an order of priority among weeds. First on the list for removal are those that are growing near and among crops. Following at a close second are perennial weeds, which must be taken out at the earliest possibility to prevent them spreading, either by underground root or overground shoot. Next come the annual weeds. These move swiftly up the order of priority, even perhaps into the top spot, when flowering and seeding threatens. The need for watering will change with the seasons and even daily, as weather conditions change. Plants that are currently flowering or that have fruit forming should have top priority within the watering hierarchy, as watering at these times will have a great impact on the quality and quantity of the crop. After these, any other plants that are obviously suffering from a lack of water should be next on the list.

General upkeep There are some jobs that, though important, can be delayed, even by a few weeks, without having too much impact on the plants. Manuring the ground is necessary to keep the soil in good condition, but this is never really an urgent job. The same goes for edging and mowing (though it will keep you happier if you put by a little time each week to weed, mow and edge at least a small area so that you are not greeted on arrival at your plot by paths all grown up to a foot and the unplanted beds all covered in weeds).

OPPOSITE Make it a priority to harvest crops at their peak, picking enough for your next few meals. BELOW In determining your priorities for watering, lavish most attention on those plants that suffer in a dry season.

TOP Where there is a mixture of annual and perennial crops, some areas will need regular digging, others not.
LEFT An onion hoe is a useful tool for close work between crops.
ABOVE Frequent additions of organic matter help to create a rich and dark, crumbly soil.

How to... a guide to a few basic jobs

Digging

Digging loosens soil that has become compacted and helps to improve soil structure so that plants get their roots down into it more easily. It is particularly useful when carried out in autumn and winter, especially on heavy soils; if the soil is dug roughly and left in large clods, frost and rain work upon it over winter to help make it more manageable. This is also a good time to add organic matter.

Single digging is a methodical approach that makes it easier to add organic matter. Decide on the area to be dug and lay a tarpaulin or large sheet of polythene at one end. Dig out a trench to spade's depth, placing the soil on to the tarpaulin. Put organic matter such as compost or well-rotted manure into the bottom of the trench, and then dig a new trench alongside the one you have just dug, turning the soil from it into the first trench. Chop up the soil in the first trench, mixing it with the organic matter.

Continue digging trenches in this way and you will progress along your designated area. When you reach the end, you will be left with a trench but no soil to fill it. Pull the tarpaulin of soil around from the other end and put it into this last trench.

Double digging is a similar technique in which you dig down to two spades' depths. This is only really necessary if you have got a problem with soil compaction, which is often the result of frequently using a rotary cultivator. This can result in poor drainage.

Creating a fine tilth

When you sow seeds it is important to create a fine tilth of soil. This means breaking the soil down into small particles so that there is always contact between the seeds and the soil. This prevents the seeds from getting dried out, as they might if they fell between large clods of earth, and it provides the best conditions for germination.

First dig over the soil thoroughly, then use a fork to break up large clods. You could then leave it for a week or so to break down further. After that, start to work on it using a rake. Rake over the surface and then use the end of the rake to tamp down any lumps of soil, before raking again. Continue this process until you have a fine, even surface.

Hoeing

Hoeing only chops the heads of weeds off and does not affect the roots at all. Because of this it is most effective on

annual weeds, which will usually be killed by this treatment, and is less so on perennial weeds, the roots of which will sprout again. Choose a hot, dry or windy day on which to hoe. In these conditions, the top growth that you chop off and any roots that are pulled up quickly become desiccated and die. In damp conditions there is always the possibility of them taking root. Take the hoe and slide it along the ground, just underneath the surface. The action should be quick and sharp, as the aim is to cut weeds rather than to pull them out. A hoe should not be used for digging into the soil to uproot weeds, although too many people use it like that – it is nowhere near as effective and will make the job take far longer. Take extra care near crop plants to make sure that you don't accidentally chop the tops off these, or damage the stems.

Hand weeding

Hand weeding is most useful around plants such as alliums that are grown fairly close together and where there is no space to run a hoe. You can simply pull up the weeds around the plants, particularly if they are annual weeds, or you can use a hand fork to dig out the roots of perennial weeds. It is important to remove as much of the root as you can, as any small amount left in the soil can sprout again.

ABOVE Sometimes there is no alternative to hand weeding. Using a hoe among closely spaced plants runs the risk of accidentally damaging the crop.
OPPOSITE Spring is one of the busiest seasons, with jobs such as erecting supports for runner beans (top left), sowing seeds (top right), planting out tomatoes (bottom right) and earthing up potatoes (bottom left).

Sample work programmes for each season

Spring

In spring there is some picking to do, but the main work is getting plants and seeds into the ground. This is a very busy time for sowing and planting, so to get the timing right make these jobs a priority. Grass and weeds are growing apace, but it is hard to keep on top of them because of the other work that needs to be done first. I make sure that I put time aside, even at this hectic time of year, to do at least a little weeding, mowing and edging every week, to prevent the plot from ever getting too overgrown and out of hand.

MONDAY: put runner bean poles up in preparation for planting (full half hour)

TUESDAY: sow runner beans (10 minutes), sow carrots (10 minutes), start digging over the ground from where overwintered cabbages have been cleared (10 minutes)

WEDNESDAY: earth up potatoes (half hour)

THURSDAY: sow salad leaves (10 minutes), tie in growing raspberry canes (10 minutes), mow a path (10 minutes)

FRIDAY: edge 5m (16ft) of paths (10 minutes), plant out tomatoes (10 minutes), weed (10 minutes)

Summer

In summer there is still some planting to do, but there is much more harvesting than earlier. Watering may become a higher priority, particularly if the weather is dry. Weeds need constant attention if they are not to become a problem, and I make sure that I allow no weeds to get to flowering and seed-setting stage. When the weather is drier, the grass grows slower than it did earlier in the year, but paths and edges still need constant attention if they are not to become overgrown.

MONDAY: dig early potatoes (10 minutes), plant out leeks (10 minutes), water (10 minutes)

TUESDAY: pick gooseberries (10 minutes), weed around carrots (10 minutes), edge 5m (16ft) of path (10 minutes)

WEDNESDAY: harvest courgettes (10 minutes), plant out cauliflowers (10 minutes), water (10 minutes)

THURSDAY: harvest French beans (10 minutes), harvest salad leaves (10 minutes), mow 5m (16ft) of path (10 minutes)

FRIDAY: harvest French beans (10 minutes), harvest salad leaves (10 minutes), mow 5m (16ft) of path (10 minutes)

BELOW Harvesting continues during autumn, with autumn-fruiting raspberries (top left) and apples (bottom right). There is also still weeding to be done (top right) and cloches to erect over salad leaves to help extend the cropping season (bottom left).

Autumn

By autumn it is all about harvesting, and I have much more time for general upkeep of the allotment than I did in spring. I start to think about how the plants are going to survive the winter, and put up protection if it is necessary. Watering is less of an issue now, particularly if there is plenty of rain. Grass and weeds are still growing, but not at the rate they were earlier in the year.

MONDAY: pick autumn raspberries (10 minutes), sow green manure on bare ground (10 minutes), cover salad leaves with cloches (10 minutes)

TUESDAY: net brassicas to protect from pigeons (20 minutes), harvest beans (10 minutes)

WEDNESDAY: weed (10 minutes), prune soft fruit bushes (20 minutes)

THURSDAY: harvest salad leaves (10 minutes), cut down summer raspberry canes and tie in new canes (20 minutes)

FRIDAY: harvest apples (10 minutes), make final cut of path edges (10 minutes), do final mow of paths (10 minutes)

Winter

In winter there is harvesting still to be done and a little planting, but the general care of the allotment – weeding, watering, edging – that has taken up so much of my time over the growing season has almost ended. It is a time to look at the plot's infrastructure, to consider any changes and to implement them, and consider what to grow the following year. It is important not to walk on or work wet soil, as you can ruin its structure. At these times there are other jobs I can be doing, such as looking at catalogues and ordering seeds.

MONDAY: harvest kale (10 minutes), prepare land for garlic planting (20 minutes)

TUESDAY: look at seed catalogues and order seeds (half hour)

WEDNESDAY: paint shed, making shed repairs (half hour)

THURSDAY: harvest leeks (10 minutes), plant out garlic (10 minutes), plant broad beans (10 minutes)

FRIDAY: harvest Brussels sprouts (10 minutes), roughly dig cleared area (20 minutes)

A cut flower garden

Dedicating an area to cut flowers goes a little beyond the strict half-hour remit, but a cut flower garden can be a wonderful addition to an allotment. It can be seen as a logical extension of the idea of growing 'dinner-party food'. Flowers, too, are at their best when fresh, and expensive to buy; as you pop up to the allotment to dig your fresh new potatoes ten minutes before your guests arrive, you can pick a vaseful of sweet peas to put on the table.

While the main reason to grow flowers at the allotment is for cutting, you may well enjoy the more colourful look they bring to the plot as well. If you are keen on having cut flowers in the house, you will have a greater and far more imaginative range of flowers to choose from if you grow your own. It is far better to grow flowers for cutting on the allotment, rather than at home in the garden. For one thing you can grow them in bulk so that you can get a really generous bunch every time, without having to put your entire garden over to tulips or daffodils, for instance. Secondly, your garden is principally for spending time in and enjoying, while the allotment's main purpose is production. With flowers growing in a garden you will be torn between wanting the garden to look good and wanting to pick flowers for the house; on the allotment there is no such dilemma, as the flowers are there to be picked.

GET ORGANIZED

Organize your cut flowers so that you have perennials and bulbs in one area, where they will be disturbed relatively rarely, and then leave space for your annuals in another area. Bulbs and perennials are best planted in rows, in order to fit as many in as possible, unless you are trying to create a garden feel to the cut flower bed.

Remember that although some plants, such as tulips, will only produce one flush of flowers per year, others like sweet peas will keep on producing new flowers as long as you keep picking them, so do this regularly. It won't really be that much of a chore.

ABOVE A tried and tested allotment favourite – deliciously scented sweet peas climb alongside runner beans. Pick the pea flowers regularly to ensure seed isn't set – once seed is formed the flowers stop being produced.

TRADITIONAL FAVOURITES

Many of the flowers traditionally grown on allotments make wonderful cut flowers. The old favourites include sweet peas (*Lathyrus odoratus* cultivars), wallflowers (*Erysimum*), gladioli, dahlias, spray chrysanthemums, daffodils (*Narcissus*) and irises. They have become associated with allotments as they are all good competition flowers that would have been primped and cosseted for the allotment or village show. These days we might not grow them for competition, but can enjoy them as they brighten up our homes instead. All benefit from growing in the big, light, open areas that are more often found on allotments than in gardens, and they love the intensive care and lack of competition. Bulbs, corms and perennial plants are particularly useful for the gardener with limited time, as they come up year after year and so need minimum attention to get them started. Among the perennials you could include roses, peonies and alchemilla, and good bulbs include daffodils, tulips, hyacinths, lilies and ornamental onions (*Allium*). All make great cut flowers.

Sweet peas

Sweet peas are a real allotment favourite, and have a wonderful scent. They must be sown from seed each year, and really need starting off early in pots under cover. Ideally they are sown in autumn to give them plenty of growing time so that the flowers arrive good and early the following summer, but you can buy plants in spring that have been started off for you. The more sweet pea flowers you pick, the more the plants will produce. This makes them worth a little extra trouble.

ANNUALS

Along with sweet peas (see box on page 107), there are a number of other annuals that are sown from seed each year and are fairly straightforward to get going.

They can be direct sown in autumn or spring. Good ones to consider for autumn or early spring sowing are cornflowers (*Centaurea cyanus*), poppies (*Papaver*), marigolds (*Calendula*), honesty (*Lunaria annua*) and scabious. Make sure you always choose hardy annuals for autumn and early spring sowing; check the seed packet instructions.

Bear in mind that some annuals, such as sweet peas, will need structures to climb up. These can be made from bamboo sticks tied together with string, or from frames of wood with pea netting strung between them. The important thing is to position them on the northernmost edge of your flower bed, so that the climbing annuals do not cast shade over the other flowers as they clamber up their structure.

When sowing annuals direct into the ground, prepare the ground well and rake it to a fine tilth. It is better to create a series of small lines into which to sow the seed, rather than just scattering it over the prepared area. Although this looks regimented at first, it will help you to distinguish the flower seeds from weed seeds as they emerge from the soil (probably at about the same time). As the flower seedlings grow you will find that they are too close to each other and you should thin them out in order to give each plant the space it needs to reach maturity and flower. Once you start to thin the rows out, they will lose their uniform look.

AN EASY CUT FLOWER GARDEN

Early autumn is a good time to start a new cut flower area, as it gives you time to put spring bulbs into place. Once you have cleared an area for growing cut flowers, dig it over well. You can leave most of the area fairly rough, to be worked on by the frosts over winter, but prepare one area well for your spring-flowering bulbs. Tulips and daffodils are good ones to start with. Plant out daffodils by mid-autumn and tulips by late autumn. Plant at least twenty bulbs of each, in rows, planting them at least three times the depth of the bulb.

In spring you can sow a few annuals. First thoroughly dig over the roughly worked ground until the soil is fine and crumbly. Then mark out little rows several inches apart and water the bottom of

these seed drills before sprinkling in seeds of easy annuals such as Shirley poppies (*Papaver rhoeas* Shirley Group cultivars), marigolds (Calendula), cornflowers (*Centaurea cyanus*) and honesty (*Lunaria annua*). As these grow, thin them out to their final spacings, which will be given on the seed packet.

Buy pots of sweet pea seedlings from a garden centre in spring, separate them and plant them out next to a sturdy frame of bamboo canes. You will need to tie them in regularly.

Spring is also the time to plant summer bulbs, corms and tubers, such as lilies, dahlias and gladioli. Plant these near the tulips and daffodils, because all these plants can stay in the ground for several years.

You should pick most flowers when the buds are just starting to open and show colour. For the longest vase life, pick them first thing in the morning if possible and place them straight in a bucket of water. If you are not going straight home, keep them in a shady place until you are ready.

ABOVE Sprinkling a packet of mixed annual seed on a corner of the plot gives a great informal mix of blooms. OVERLEAF Bright, bold and beautiful: an eye-catching block of flowers in hot colours livens up the view.

THE FIRST
YEAR

The first year on your allotment is a critical time. You have enthusiasm on your side, but the majority of people who abandon their allotments do so during this period. It is essential that you approach this crucial time with the right attitude. The most important thing to remember is that you can't do everything; give yourself a break and don't expect to win Best Plot this first year. There will be times when your plot looks messy, when it doesn't come up to the standard of those around you and when favourite crops fail to flourish. Don't beat yourself up about it.

TARGETS FOR YOUR FIRST YEAR

You need to be realistic about what you can do, and a good target to aim for is to get one-third of your plot weed-free and planted up by the end of the year. Whatever size of plot you have, this should give you enough space to get plenty of salad crops and a few other bits and pieces out of it and make you feel like a proper allotment gardener, but one-third is still a small enough area to be attainable and easily kept under control once cleared. It will give you an area where you can practise your techniques before you start your onslaught on the whole plot.

RIGHT Concentrate on cultivating just a part of your allotment to start with. One-third of the plot is a realistic target.

When to start?

For new allotment holders, particularly those with little experience of gardening, some time in mid-spring is probably the best time to start. Horny old gardeners will tell you to get on to your new plot and start digging in mid-winter, and it is true that getting some land cleared then will give you a head start. But winter can be grim and off-putting, and there is little point in making life hard for yourself. In winter there is much time when the ground is wet and should not be worked because of the possibility of compacting it and ruining its structure. By mid-spring the weather is starting to warm up, and it is much more pleasant to be outside; rather than dreading the cold and rain, you will find yourself longing to get up to your plot and out into the open air.

Get growing

Although it is important, in the long run, to grow your crops in different places each year as part of a rotation plan (more on this on pages 151–3), the first year is not the time to worry about this. You will be desperate to get something into the ground and growing, and that is exactly what you should do. As soon as an area is clear of weeds, plant it up. Making a rough note of where each crop went in the first year will be helpful when deciding what to plant where in subsequent years, but that is really as much as you need do about crop rotation for now.

You will pour much of your energy in your first year into getting the weeds under control, and mid-spring is the time when weeds start actively growing.

It may surprise you, but this actually makes them easier to control; some are not even visible until they start growing, because they die down under the soil over winter, while most are hit harder by the various weed control methods once they have put on a bit of soft, lush growth. The sun and wind of a typical spring day is the perfect drying environment, and any weed roots that are exposed on such a day will be quickly desiccated and killed.

WEED CLEARANCE

When attempting any of these methods of clearing weeds, it is a good idea to force yourself to stick to the half-hour system and do a little each day. You will see far more consistent results and will avoid putting your back out.

Digging out

The simplest, most backbreaking method is simply to dig the weeds out. It can be painfully slow if you want to do it really well, but it is pretty effective. Although it will get rid of most weeds, there will be some pernicious perennial weeds that you cannot get every last bit of: you will always end up leaving little bits of roots in the ground that will spring back into life. You should be prepared to come back and dig these up again.

OPPOSITE Make a start by getting at least part of your plot dug over and ready for planting (top left). As soon as you have cleared an area, waste no time in getting a crop planted and growing (top right)
ABOVE Little and often is the key to taking the backbreak out of digging.

Turning the soil

A combination of digging out the worst weeds and simply turning the rest of the plot over can be effective. By turning the soil you will expose the worst of the roots, allowing them to dry out. If you have heavy soil, it will expose it to the elements, which help it to break down, and you will be able to come along at a later date and pick out many of the roots with the soil in a far more workable condition. Turning the soil just once is not enough, though: to clear the ground you will have to do it repeatedly, digging out all the roots of weeds as you go. For the best results, choose a spring day when there is sun and wind, which will cause the dug roots to dry out rapidly.

Covering the soil

Excluding light from the weeds will eventually kill them, and this can be achieved by placing a thick, light-excluding layer over the ground. First, you should use a rotary trimmer over the whole area to cut the weeds down to a manageable size (you may be able to borrow a trimmer from a neighbour or friend, or you could try a tool hire shop). Try to dig out any large, woody weeds, such as brambles, which will prevent you from getting a good, flat surface.

Once you have the area roughly cut and levelled, lay your light-excluding mulch. You will need to do a good job of this, making sure that every inch is well covered, as opportunistic weeds will seize upon any chinks of light. Ideally, you should leave this mulch on the ground until it kills all the weeds beneath it and they rot down into the soil.

Beware the mechanical cultivator

A mechanical cultivator is a powered machine that has two circular blades that churn through the soil, slicing into it. It is used for 'clearing' plots because it has an instant impact: after a few hours' work you have what looks like a beautifully cleared plot with a lot less effort than digging. This is deceptive. If there are any perennial weeds at all in the soil, the cultivator will cut them up into many tiny pieces and spread these all over the plot. Pernicious weeds have earned their reputation because they are able to regenerate from the tiniest piece of root, and so all you do by cutting them up is propagate them and spread them around. Added to this, frequent use of a cultivator can lead to soil compaction and problems with drainage. Refuse all offers of the loan of a cultivator until you are sure that you have got rid of all perennial weeds.

The best material to use is cardboard, weighted down with stones, as it is thick enough to exclude light but relatively quick to decompose and disappear into the soil. If you find that weeds grow through the cardboard, you may need to add another layer. Alternatively you could use layers of newspaper, although these are harder to control, particularly when laying them. Black plastic is often used, as it forms a permanent barrier to light, but it makes an ideal hiding place for slugs and snails.

The main problem with the light-excluding method is the amount of time it takes. Killing the weeds will take at least a year, and two would be better. It can be carried out at any time of the year; usually the sooner you do it the better. However, if you are considering this method in late winter or early spring, wait until the weeds are actively growing. Many, particularly those that die down over winter such as bindweed, will have stored reserves of energy at the end of the previous summer to get them through the winter and early

spring until they have made enough growth to start photosynthesizing and supporting themselves again. If you can put the mulch down just after this first flush of growth, you will deprive them of this vital injection of solar energy just when they are at their most vulnerable.

ABOVE Potatoes are an excellent crop for helping to clear weedy ground. The act of digging them up and their spreading root system helps break up the soil.

Removing the surface of the soil

If your plot is covered almost entirely in couch grass, you might find it easiest simply to remove the top layer of turf and soil, and either stack it grass side down to exclude the light, or cover it with a light-suppressing cover. The couch grass will eventually die and rot down, leaving you with a beautiful pile of topsoil and well-rotted organic matter to use on your plot. Taking off the top layer will not remove all the roots, and you will have to dig the remainder out, but it will get rid of the worst of them and leave the rest exposed and easy to get at.

Using other plants to keep the weeds down

Weeds get out of hand on abandoned plots partly because they have no competition. Simply growing other plants on your plot will help you to keep weeds under control. It is disheartening to clear an area and then return a couple of weeks later to find that it is covered in weeds and you have to start all over again. The best way to avoid this is to plant something in each spot as soon as you have cleared it, as that way you will have more of an incentive to keep the area clear of weeds. You are more likely to pop back and hoe regularly while you wait for your seeds to germinate or your plants to get established than you are to bother to keep up a blank piece of land – and the weeds will have some competition.

Help from potatoes

If you have a particularly weedy piece of ground, removing the worst of the weeds and then planting it with potatoes (maincrop or new) can be a great way of clearing it. Any ground that is continually dug over will become progressively easier to work, and earthing up potatoes as they grow to prevent the new tubers from turning green in the sunlight achieves this. The simple action of turning the soil loosens weed roots from their hold and exposes them, and the fact that it is repeated several times through the growing season seems to be enough to knock many weeds back. The large root systems of potatoes mean that much of the soil is broken up beyond what you have been turning. The following year you will find an area where potatoes have been planted to be the part of your plot that is the most weed-free, with the most easily worked soil.

Other vegetables with particularly good weed-suppressing qualities include cabbages, pumpkins and courgettes. Their large leaves block out a huge amount of light over a long period of time and this prevents the weeds from thriving beneath them. The roots break the soil up well, and after cropping you will find it crumbly and in great condition.

Getting rid of the weeds is only the first step in bringing your allotment into good, productive condition. Once you have cleared the ground, you are likely to find that your soil still needs some attention before you start sowing and planting your crops. There is more information on getting the best from your soil in chapter 7.

MANAGING YOUR FALLOW AREA

You will be itching to get started on your cultivated third, where you can get plants in and start the more exciting side of allotmenting. However, getting a grip on your fallow two-thirds is equally important. If you leave it in the state you find it, it will quickly turn into a messy, morale-sapping eyesore.

You can manage this rough two-thirds in different ways. You could remove the larger weeds and then rotary trim the whole plot, before setting up a regular mowing regime as part of your half-hour timetable. Regular mowing is incredibly effective at killing most weeds; being cut down to the ground each time they are about to start a growth spurt can be fatal for all sorts of weeds, including docks, nettles, bracken and thistles. Eventually you will be left with an area of grass that is relatively easy to care for. Or you could use the year that you are going to let this area lie fallow to your advantage and use thelight-excluding method described on pages 118–120. This will make the two-thirds much easier to clear once you are ready to start on it during your second year.

Green manures

If you do not have seeds or plants ready to go into your freshly cleared ground, consider sowing a green manure. Green manures are particularly useful if you have cleared some ground in autumn that you are not planning to plant up until spring, but they can be used any time you plan to leave a piece of ground bare for over six weeks. Sown thickly over the ground, they germinate quickly and smother emerging weeds. Before they flower and set seed, they are turned into the soil and left to rot. As they rot down, they add bulky organic matter, which helps to improve the structure of the soil. They also help prevent erosion of soil nutrients and can even add nutrients to the soil.

Suitable seeds are usually sold simply as 'green manures' but include

- lupins
- grazing rye
- alfalfa
- mustard
- field beans
- clover

OPPOSITE Green manures are useful for spare areas of cleared ground. Plants such as yellow-flowered mustard and various legumes are sown thickly and the young plants are turned into the soil before they flower.

ABOVE LEFT Making your plot look well cared for by trimming edges and cutting grass paths neatly will help to make a good impression on your fellow allotmenteers.
OPPOSITE A touch of humour on the plot always helps to keep your gardening neighbours friendly!
OVERLEAF On a large allotment site with lots of people holding plots alongside each other it makes all the difference if everybody is on good terms.

GETTING ALONG WITH YOUR NEIGHBOURS

If you take on a plot on an allotment site, one of the most daunting parts of getting started can be your neighbours. Many people will be lucky and have supportive and encouraging allotmenteers on neighbouring plots. Even so, the sight of a perfectly manicured allotment on either side of yours can lower your morale, and some neighbours can be critical, particularly of slow progress.

The best advice, of course, is to ignore such intrusions and stick to your plan, but this can be easier said than done. Be friendly to your neighbours, and ask their advice if you need it, but there may come a point when you have to keep your head down and get on with your work.

The one thing that will alienate you most from neighbouring plot holders is an overgrown weedy plot, and this is why the management of your fallow patch is of such importance. If you have cleared away any rubbish and are cutting your fallow patch regularly, they will have no reason to be concerned.

A final neighbour-impressing tip is to make sure that you always cut your grass paths and trim your edges. This is the nearest you can get to cheating: it is amazing the difference ten minutes' trimming can make, even if all within is utterly chaotic.

NURTURING YOUR PLANTS

You may get great results at first simply by sowing or planting out direct into the soil and hoping for the best. But the time will come when some problem or other will hit you: the soil may be leaching nutrients, or your plants may get struck by frost or pushed over by the wind. You will make your allotment more productive and easier to manage if you learn how to nurture your soil and crops.

TREATING THE SOIL

The soil is your greatest asset. It will pay to spend some time getting to know the soil on your plot, and giving it some basic treatments, should that prove necessary (it nearly always does). Some basic amelioration can unlock the hidden potential of your soil, turning it from a lumpen mass that produces miserable crops to an easily worked, crumbly soil that gives prize-winning yields.

One of the things you should try to do early on is find out exactly what type of soil you have. This will affect the kinds of crops you can grow, and the level of success you can expect. However, a poor soil is not terminal. There are also things that you can do, fairly easily, to make changes to the soil that will increase its workability and productivity.

Assessing the soil

Allotment soil can be dreadful. It has often been overworked, compacted and neglected over many generations and the result can be a ruined soil with an overly fine surface that becomes 'capped' in dry weather, which means that a fine layer of soil particles melds together, forming a layer over the soil that prevents water from penetrating. This is why it is sometimes better, despite the extra work involved, to go for a plot that has been abandoned for a while where at least the soil has had a chance to recover from intensive cropping.

You should be able to assess your soil's basic make-up just by digging it and getting your hands into it. The three main types are clay soil, silty soil and sandy soil. Most soils are a combination of these, and the physical and chemical properties of a soil depend on their relative proportions.

Clay soil: A soil that is predominantly made up of clay is heavy and holds a lot of moisture; you will find it almost impossible to dig after rain because of this. When you dig it, it will come out in big clods, and the spade may leave a shiny surface. Pick a bit up and feel it between your fingers. It will be smooth and cool to touch. It can be easily moulded and will hold its shape.

Sandy soil: A predominantly sandy soil is much easier to dig, and you will notice that water drains away very quickly after rain. When you pick some up, it will feel gritty to the touch, and it will not form into a ball.

Silty soil: Soils that are made up mostly of silt particles feel silky when rubbed between the fingers and they retain moisture a little better than sandy soils.

If you are very lucky you will have loam, which is a good balance of clay, sand and silt. This is easy to dig, crumbly, and drains and holds water well, and it forms into a soft ball that will disintegrate easily. It is, unfortunately, fairly rare.

Benefits and drawbacks

There are benefits and drawbacks to each of these soils. Clay soil can be slow to warm up in spring, which delays sowing times, and it can be hard to work. However, it holds water and nutrients well, making it particularly fertile. Once plants are established you may not need to water, as there is always moisture available in the soil. It is a particularly good soil for growing plants that appreciate a good fertility, such as fruit trees and brassicas, but you will struggle to grow crops that need really good drainage, such as Mediterranean herbs, or those that need easy access through the soil, such as root crops. Sandy soils warm up quickly in spring but their free-draining nature means that nutrients are easily washed through and they can dry out more quickly than clay soils. Silty soils are vulnerable to compaction.

Adding organic matter

The good thing is that each type of soil needs much the same treatment to improve it. Lots of organic matter – in the form of well-rotted farmyard manure, garden compost or green manures – dug into any soil will improve its structure. Organic matter breaks up the dense, closely packed particles of clay soil, allowing small gaps where air can get in and water can drain out. But it coats the large, loose soil particles of sandy soil

and knits them together, helping them to hold on to water and nutrients.

Many forms of organic matter contain nutrients, but it is best not to rely on these to feed your plants and to use them primarily as a way of improving structure. That way you can dig them into the soil in autumn or winter, or just lay them on top of the soil in autumn, giving the weather and the worms time to work them well into the soil, without worrying about nutrients leaching out in winter rains. Never use fresh manure, as the ammonia in it can harm plants (and it smells horrible). If you are having manure delivered, ask how long

ABOVE The addition of well-rotted organic matter such as manure or garden compost will improve all types of soil.

it has been left to rot. If it is fresh, you will need to create an area on your plot where you can cover it and leave it for a year to mature before you start applying it to the soil.

Acid or alkaline?

The pH of the soil is a measure, on a scale of 0 to 14, of how acidic or alkaline it is. An acid soil will have a pH below 7, and an alkaline soil will have one above 7. Most vegetables grow best in a fairly neutral soil; the ideal is approximately 6.5, with anything between 5.7 and 6.8 being acceptable. The problem with an excessively high or low pH is that both can 'lock out' nutrients, so that even if nutrients are present in the soil in large quantities, plants can't access them and so do not grow as vigorously as they should, resulting in lower yields.

If your soil is too acidic (the pH is too low), this is pretty easy to remedy with applications of lime (see box). Making your soil less alkaline (by reducing the pH) is more tricky. If you find that the pH of your soil is high, the best thing to do is plant into it as it is, since most vegetables can tolerate a relatively high pH. The process of continuous cropping and cultivation, along with the chemical action of rain, will gradually lower the pH. Do not add mushroom composts to alkaline or neutral soils, as these products often contain chalk, which can lead to an increase in pH. Conversely, such composts would be useful on acidic soils.

FEEDING

If your plot has been left fallow, you will probably find that there is little benefit in feeding your plants for the first year or so, but if it has been heavily cropped you may need to apply some fertilizer to the soil to replace the nutrients removed by the previous crops.

All fertilizers are made up of a combination of three main nutrients which plants need in large quantities,

Test your soil

It is essential to find out your soil's pH level early on. This may sound complicated and scientific but there are simple and inexpensive tests that you can buy from garden centres. You simply add your soil to the tube of solution in the pack, then use a colour chart to match the colour of the solution to a pH level. It is a very simple test to carry out and will be a sound investment, as knowing the results can make a huge difference to your crops. You will need to repeat the pH test each year, as the pH level can gradually change, depending on what you add to the soil.

The miracle of lime

Lime is sold in a powdered form which is spread all over the soil before being roughly dug in. It is worth bypassing the small boxes sold in garden centres and heading for the allotment shop, if you have one. Such a shop will sell it by the hundredweight, and this is the sort of quantity in which you will need to apply it if it is to make any difference (it is incredibly cheap, even in these quantities). Apply lime in spring, and then watch your crops grow to almost miraculous proportions as they unlock all the hidden potential in your soil. Lime is also a secret weapon in the war against clay soil, as it can help to break it down and make it more workable.

OPPOSITE Once you start to dig over a newly acquired plot you will be able to assess what type of soil you have.

OPPOSITE TOP Organic matter is vital for healthy soil. You may be able to get sacks of well-rotted manure or similar delivered to your plot.
OPPOSITE BOTTOM LEFT Plants in the pea and bean family have nodules on their roots that capture nitrogen from the air to use as food.
OPPOSITE BOTTOM RIGHT An application of lime can help to release nutrients that are locked up in the soil, making them available to plants.

each of which encourages a particular type of growth.

- Nitrogen (N) is the nutrient that is most needed by the majority of vegetables, and it encourages lots of leafy top growth.
- Phosphorus (P) is particularly good for encouraging root growth.
- Potassium (K) helps to ensure good flowering and fruit formation.

All plants need a combination of these three nutrients, plus lots of micronutrients, to survive and grow well, but each needs them in varying quantities depending on the part of the plant (leaf, root or fruit) that is to be cropped. The abbreviations N, P and K are commonly used on fertilizer packaging, and the N:P:K ratio shows how much of each is present in the product.

As long as the soil is relatively fertile, only nitrogen is likely to be lacking, although you could consider applying a potassium-rich fertilizer for fruiting crops such as tomatoes and peppers. A general fertilizer that is high in nitrogen would do well by most crops, and the pelleted forms of chicken manure and seaweed that are widely available seem to be among the most effective at getting the nitrogen to the plants in a form that they can use.

Organic or inorganic?

Inorganic or artificial fertilizers, such as sulphate of ammonia or potash, or the general fertilizer Growmore, tend to be fast-acting. The nutrients reach the plant quickly, but the effect may be short-lived. Organic fertilizers, such as fish, blood and bone, or pelleted chicken manure, often contain more micronutrients and act more slowly; they also promote the activity of beneficial soil organisms, such as bacteria, which are required to convert the fertilizer particles into a form that plants can absorb.

WATERING

Watering is a necessity on all allotments, but the amount you will need to do will vary dramatically depending on your soil and local climate. Plants grown on a clay soil in a damp part of the country may only need watering in when they are planted out or sown, while the same crop on a sandy soil in a dry area will need daily watering at certain times of the year.

Generally, the more water you can give your crops the better they will be. Even before the edible parts are formed, water will help the plants to grow large and healthy, and that will improve the quality and quantity of your crops. However, if time is short, with certain crops you can improve cropping most significantly by watering at particular stages of their development. This will usually be when the crop part of the plant is forming. Potato tubers form when the plants start flowering, so you should give the plants extra water then. With fruiting plants, such as raspberries, the key watering time is when the fruits are swelling. Lettuce, courgettes, sweet corn, melons, aubergines and French and runner beans benefit from lots of water, and should be watered as often as you can manage. Brassicas, on the other hand, do not really need watering once they are established, and will produce great crops without any extra input. Carrots also need very little watering once they have germinated.

How to water well

There is a bit of a knack to watering; you can't just splash it around any old how,

Dust mulch

You can reduce the amount of water you need to use by creating a 'dust mulch'. This is a technique used in the Mediterranean. It is particularly useful on clay soils, which crack in dry weather, creating large chasms down which water disappears and making it almost impossible to water efficiently. The idea is to create a fine tilth on the surface of the soil around the plants, and to maintain it with constant hoeing. Cracks never get the chance to form and watering is straightforward.

OPPOSITE TOP The most efficient time to water plants is in the evening, when you are less likely to lose water to evaporation.
OPPOSITE BOTTOM If the tap is a long walk from your plot, save yourself time by buying two cans and filling them both on each trip.

at any time. Well, you can, but if you do you will lose lots of water through evaporation, and you may do some damage to the plants. The best time to water is in the evening. At this time the temperature will be dropping and so the water is less likely to disappear into the atmosphere and more likely to end up getting right down to the roots of the plant. In summer you may need to leave watering as late as 7pm. Another reason to wait until then is the damage that the combination of heat and water can do to plant leaves: droplets that fall on leaves can heat up, particularly if they are in direct sunlight, and the heat can leave scorch marks. A final reason to water later during warm weather is that hauling a couple of watering cans around is less exhausting in the cool of the evening than it is in the middle of the day.

The technique for watering all crops is the same: try to water the soil rather

than the plant. Even in the evening water on leaves can be a problem, as it sits on the leaves and cools and may encourage moulds to form. Don't use a rose to water anything other than freshly sown seeds and seedlings (lettuces in particular will rot within a few days if you water all over their leaves with a rose). Get the spout as close to the base of the plant as you can. If you notice that water is just running off the surface of the soil, bank up a small amount of soil to create a circular ridge around the plant. This will prevent immediate run-off and keep the water in place long enough for it to soak down to the roots. The capillary action of moist soil makes it much easier to water than soil

that has baked hard, so if you water every day you will probably get much less of a problem with water running off the surface, and will need to use less water than you would if you watered less frequently.

PROVIDING SUPPORT

Creating adequate support for your plants will prevent potential disasters. There is nothing worse than nurturing a plant all through the year and then finding that its flimsy support has collapsed at the crucial moment, ruining your entire crop.

Whenever you are planting tall crops, consider the direction of the prevailing wind before deciding in what direction

the rows should run. (If you do not know in what direction your prevailing wind blows, ask other allotment holders, or buy – or even make – a cheap wind vane for your plot.) Commercial growers always plant a couple of sacrificial rows on the windward side of their crops. These act as windbreaks for the rest of the plants but seldom produce high-quality fruit. On an allotment, you do not have the space to allow you that luxury, but you can bear the principle in mind. Planting the rows at right angles to the prevailing wind will mean that all the plants will receive its full force, and this will lead to poorer-quality crops and make it more likely that the supports will give way in sudden gusts.

Instead, plant the rows so that they run in the same direction as the wind. This way the wind receives the minimum resistance and so is less likely to push the supports over; and only the last couple of plants on each row become sacrificial, rather than all of them.

OPPOSITE Tall-growing or climbing plants such as peas need sturdy supports that will not collapse under the weight of the crop.
ABOVE LEFT On a windy plot, sow crop rows running in the same direction as the prevailing wind, not at right angles to it.
ABOVE RIGHT Mounding soil up slightly round the bases of top-heavy plants, particularly brassicas, will help keep them stable and upright.

Types of support

There are two main categories of support: those that are for permanent plants and those for annuals. The former must be really sturdy. Raspberries are a case in point. Their long, whippy growth can reach up to 2m (7ft) in height, and their leaves expand to create plenty of wind resistance. On an exposed plot this can be a lethal combination. Support for raspberries needs to be much more sturdy than you might at first imagine. These plants will be in the same spot for many years, so build the support to last. You can make a good start by getting hold of some good-quality tree stakes made of something solid and water-resistant such as chestnut wood. Pine is no use, as it will quickly rot away. Position one at either end of your row and string strong wire between them, which the raspberries can be tied to as they grow. The same style of support can be used for cordon-grown redcurrants, blackcurrants and gooseberries.

You will need to construct temporary supports each year for crops such as climbing beans and peas. Permanent supports would be no good for these crops, as they would prevent you from using the ground after the crops were over and from moving the crop from place to place each year. The most commonly used support for climbing beans is a double row of bamboo canes, tied together at the top. This is as good a system as any, so long as it is done well. Buy the highest quality, thickest bamboo canes you can find, making sure that they are good and long, at least 2.5m (8ft). Push them into the ground about 38cm (15in) apart on either side of the row, leaning towards each other. At each end of the row make a tripod of canes, to give the whole structure stability, and make another tripod in the middle of the row. Then join the whole thing together by placing more canes horizontally in the 'V' formed where the canes meet at the top, and tying them in at each point. String tied between all the canes lower down will provide extra stability and give climbing plants something to cling to.

Peas and mange tout are traditionally supported with pea sticks. These are twiggy branches, often cut from hazel, although they can be from any tree that has fine, twiggy growth. They are pushed into the ground next to the pea seedling, which then clambers up through the twigs. They are an excellent support as long as they are long enough to push firmly into the ground. If you do not have access to any

suitable branches, a coarse piece of netting strung between two sturdy supports is very effective.

Tomatoes are usually supported with bamboo canes, which are woefully inadequate. As these plants often end up with many heavy bunches of fruit hanging from them, they really need a sturdy stake. In this case pine will do, as the plants will not be left in the ground year on year.

PROVIDING PROTECTION FROM FROST

During the main growing season you will not have to consider frost protection, but if you extend the season into early spring or autumn, you will run the risk of losing precious seedlings and young plants to frost, or frost damaging plants with the result that they take longer to crop or produce lower-quality vegetables.

There are some plants that you will need to plant out fairly early in the year, at a time when frosts may or may not have passed. Early potatoes are a good example. They are usually planted in mid-spring, when there is still a definite threat of cold snaps. In their case, soil is an effective insulation. The parts of the potato that are under the ground are unlikely to be affected by the light frosts of early spring, so if you earth up the soil as they grow, you should not have a problem. You will need to give other early crops more protection by covering the bed with a double layer of horticultural fleece or perforated clear plastic. Pin down the edges of the fleece by tucking them into a slit trench made by a spade. Straw, grass mowings and even old cabbage leaves can also be spread over the soil to similar effect, but this may not protect the growing tips of some plants.

OPPOSITE (Top) A double row of canes is given stability by tying more canes horizontally along the top of the row. Victorian-style cloches (bottom left) are attractive and useful for protecting individual plants, but tunnels covered with horticultural fleece (bottom right) are cheaper and more practical.

Extend the season with cloches

If you would like to be more proactive in your extension of the season, consider investing in some lightweight, moveable cloches. These are not cheap, but will be a great investment, and far easier to use than some Heath-Robinsonesque contraption made from skip finds. Buy a set of decent-sized ones, at least 45cm (18in) high, in order to get the full range of uses out of them. The main purpose of cloches is to give plants some protection over winter. Placed over the soil, they provide enough protection to allow crops such as spinach and carrots to keep actively growing, almost throughout winter. This means that rather than relying on the old, tough carrots that grew the previous season you can have young and relatively tender ones.

They also provide the perfect spot for winter salad leaves. Used at the beginning of spring, they can bring back the sowing times of a huge range of vegetables, as you can leave them on until the frosts have passed, and when you remove them the plants will already be well established and ready to take off. Another use is for more subtropical vegetables such as aubergines and melons during summer. These are not reliable out of doors in cool climates or in areas with short summers, where a cloche will provide that little extra heat and make all the difference.

COMPOSTING

Composting is an essential part of allotmenting. Not only does it produce lots of organic matter with which to improve your soil, but it is also the best way

Hit the bottle

Plastic bottles, cut in half and pushed into the soil over individual plants, can be a good way of nursing young plants through early, frost-prone times. They keep frosts at bay and can deter slugs, but come with a caution: take care to remove them before the leaves touch the sides, as frost will burn any touching parts.

of disposing of the huge amounts of green waste that are produced by the average allotment. At its simplest, composting means combining all your waste and leaving it to rot down, but there is a little more to it if you want to prevent it from turning into a gooey mess that sits for years without rotting down properly.

Choosing a bin

The first thing you need to consider is which compost bin to go for. Cheap plastic compost bins are perfectly serviceable; if you are happy to spend a little more money, you can buy ones with openings at the base, which allow access to the rotted-down material while the stuff on the top is still fresh. There are also lots of recycled materials that can be put to great use as compost bins; four pallets nailed together makes one of the most effective. If you buy or make something that is mobile, you can move it each time a load of compost is ready. This way you just remove the structure, spread the compost over the nearby area, then move the bin to a new

position, creating one extremely well-composted area at a time.

Whether you make your own or buy something in, make sure that you get one that is generously sized and lets a little air in but is not too open. Some people use four stakes for the four corners and just wrap chicken wire around them, but this lets in a little too much air and the heap will dry out too quickly. One of the best systems is a set of three wooden compost bins (bought or home-made makes no difference). The reason for three is that it allows you to turn the compost from one bin to another, and this is one of the keys to producing good compost quickly. You start filling the second bin when the first is full, and use the spare one as space to turn the first into. Eventually you should get a constant supply of good compost.

The secret of good composting

So what are the secrets of composting? The trick is to get a good mix of ingredients. If you put in only grass clippings or soft, leafy material, the heap will soon get slimy. If it is all dry, woody material, the heap will not start to rot down at all. A combination of the two is perfect. If your heap is getting slimy and you have no dryer material to add, throw in some shredded or scrunched-up newspaper and stir the heap up to incorporate it. If it is too dry, water it and cover it with a lid or a piece of carpet to keep moisture in and help keep the heap warm. The smaller the pieces of

ABOVE If your budget isn't limited, you can buy from a wide range of efficient compost bins and temporary weed-suppressing mulches which will make life easier.

waste are, the quicker they will rot down. The perfect solution is to shred all waste through a garden shredder before adding it to the heap, but if you do not have one, simply chop up any larger pieces. Constant turning of the heap not only speeds up the composting process but prevents your heap becoming a home to compost flies. These flies lay their eggs in the top layer of freshly added material, so if you cover the new additions with old, more rotted-down stuff, they will not get access to them and will be less of a problem.

There are a few things you should not add to your compost heap.

- **Woody items** Anything too woody, such as cabbage and broccoli stalks, will take too long to rot down, unless they are well shredded.
- **Diseased material** You must avoid composting anything with any sign of disease. Composting onion tops contaminated with white rot, for example, would result in you spreading white rot spores over the whole plot with the compost. Similarly, it is a good idea to avoid adding any potato tops, as these can often contain potato blight spores.
- **Perennial weeds** Never compost any parts of perennial weeds. Many can resprout from even the tiniest piece, and you will end up spreading the weed across the plot when you next dig your compost into the soil.

Making leafmould

Leafmould makes a superb soil conditioner and mulch, but tree leaves do not make good additions to a compost heap, as they take such a long time to rot down. If you have lots of them, it is best to make a separate leafmould bin for them. This can be very simple – just a cage made of wire netting. Fill the bin and just wait for the leaves to decompose to lovely, dark, crumbly leafmould.

ROTATION

Rotation is the practice of moving each group of crops from one area to another each year. This helps to prevent the diseases and pests of each crop from building up in the soil, as they would if that crop were grown year after year in the same area. You should aim for a minimum of a four-year rotation. This means that you will need four separate beds, and that each type of crop will not be grown in the same area for four years. The main groups of crops that are considered as part of a rotation plan are as follows: beans and peas, root crops (including potatoes), brassicas and onions.

Planning your rotation

There are all sorts of rules you can follow in order to decide which crops should follow which, but these are the finer points. If you can make sure that the same crop does not grow in the same place year on year, you are halfway to winning the battle. That said, the qualities and growth habits of each crop can be used to the advantage of the following crop, and so it can pay to bear these in mind when choosing an order for your rotation. For instance, peas and beans are very good at fixing nitrogen from the air. Nitrogen becomes concentrated in nodules in their roots, and if these are snipped off and dug into the soil when the plants have finished cropping, the nitrogen will become available to the next crop put into that ground. Brassicas are particularly heavy feeders, so they make a good follow-on crop from peas and beans. Potatoes are good at clearing the ground of weeds, mainly because they are earthed up so regularly, but also because they are very leafy, and so shade out weeds. Seedlings that are tricky to weed, such as those of onions, are a good follow-on crop.

Each crop will benefit from slightly different soil treatment before it is sown or planted out. The area where brassicas are to be planted should be limed, as this helps to prevent club root. Brassicas may also benefit from an application of manure. Root crops such as carrots and parsnips should not be planted into areas that have been recently manured because manure can cause the roots to fork. Onions, too, should not go into freshly manured soil, as there is a link between fresh manure and white rot.

If you get any recurring disease or pest problems, extend your rotation cycle to make it as long as possible. Some diseases and pests can stay in the soil for many years, so the longer you can make your rotation, the more chance you have of starving out your particular problem, even if you can only extend the rotation for the one problem crop.

You will notice that some commonly grown allotment crops, such as pumpkins, courgettes and salad crops, are not included in the above information on rotation. This is mainly because they do not have too many problems and can be fitted in wherever there is space among the other crops.

It is not always easy to practise a perfect rotation. For one thing, it means generally allocating the same amount of space to each of the crops, though you may not want as many onions as brassicas. This is where the crops mentioned above that are not included in the rotation plan can be useful in filling gaps. As a precaution, however, avoid planting even these crops in the same spot every year.

OPPOSITE Rotating groups of crops helps to avoid pests and disease problems and depleting the soil of nutrients.

FOUR-BED CROP ROTATION PLAN

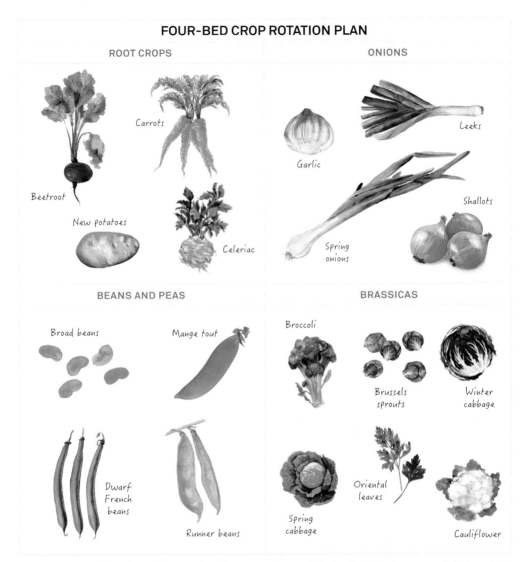

ROOT CROPS

Carrots

Beetroot

New potatoes

Celeriac

ONIONS

Garlic

Leeks

Shallots

Spring onions

BEANS AND PEAS

Broad beans

Mange tout

Dwarf French beans

Runner beans

BRASSICAS

Broccoli

Brussels sprouts

Winter cabbage

Spring cabbage

Oriental leaves

Cauliflower

The four crop groups (above) should be rotated on a four-year cycle around Plot A to Plot D. The four-year cycle is shown in the table below.

NB: Cucurbits (such as courgettes, melons and squash) as well as sweet corn can be grown in any of the beds where it is convenient. Other non-rotational crops that are perennial or permanent include apples, pears, strawberries, raspberries, loganberries and other hybrid berries, redcurrants, rhubarb and asparagus.

	PLOT A	PLOT B	PLOT C	PLOT D
YEAR ONE	Root crops	Onions	Beans and peas	Brassicas
YEAR TWO	Brassicas	Root crops	Onions	Beans and peas
YEAR THREE	Beans and peas	Brassicas	Root crops	Onions
YEAR FOUR	Onions	Beans and peas	Brassicas	Root crops

MANAGING PESTS AND DISEASES

Pests and diseases can have a devastating effect on an allotment. They can cause havoc among your vegetables, reducing yields and ruining quality. Many old-school allotmenteers swear by chemical controls, but as laws on pesticide use become more stringent there are fewer chemicals available to the allotment gardener, and you may wish to avoid the use of synthetic chemicals anyway. It can be simpler and, in the long run, less time consuming to take a more holistic approach. The most important factor in keeping problems at bay is to get your plants growing strongly so that they have all their natural defences about them; that way they will be well equipped to withstand any pest and disease attack.

Keep plants strong

Soil is the key to growing strong plants. If plants cannot get their roots properly down into the soil because it is compacted, if they meet waterlogging, or if they cannot extract enough nutrients or water from the soil, they get stressed and become more vulnerable to attack. A good system of rotation is also essential, so that pests and diseases never get a chance to really get a foothold in one area. If you have been rotating crops, digging your soil over, improving it with organic matter, feeding it and adjusting its acidity or alkalinity according to the needs of your vegetables, you will not be able to help having good, healthy plants, and this will give you a serious head start on their attackers. You want to reach the stage where you need only put the minimum amount of effort into controlling pests and diseases.

However, some problems will sneak past even the best plant defences and for these there are other approaches to complement hearty growth. Take some time to experiment with a few different ways in which to reduce the damage caused by pests and diseases, to see what works best for you. By getting a good balance of all of these methods you will develop a plot that has its own balance of predators and pests, and this will allow you to spend less time on each individual problem.

RESISTANT CULTIVARS

One of the greatest weapons in the fight against pests and diseases is the use of resistant cultivars. These plants have been specifically bred to resist attack by particular pests or diseases. They are no guarantee, but chances are that if a pest is given a choice between a resistant cultivar and an ordinary one, the former will fare best. If you have a recurrent problem with a particular pest or disease, always try to track down a cultivar that promises some resistance to it.

A few examples of resistant varieties are:
- root aphid-resistant lettuces – 'Little Gem', 'Barcelona', 'Avondefiance'
- blight-resistant tomatoes – 'Ferline'
- blight-resistant potatoes – 'Blue Danube', 'Lady Balfour', 'Sarpo Axona', 'Sarpo Mira'
- slug-resistant potatoes – 'Accent', 'Foremost', 'Kestrel', 'Sante'
- carrot fly-resistant carrots – 'Resistafly', 'Flyaway'
- clubroot-resistant Brussels sprouts – 'Crispus', 'Cronus'
- rust-resistant leeks – 'Porbella', 'Below Zero'

COMPANION PLANTING

There are many different reasons for companion planting. The most common are to confuse pests in one way or another, and to encourage beneficial insects, which

ABOVE Marigolds planted among crops are thought to deter many insect pests that locate their target by scent.
OPPOSITE Strong-smelling onions growing among carrots will help to confuse carrot flies, literally putting them off the scent.

may predate on garden pests. Planting crops in large monocultures, as commercial farmers do, suits pests and diseases perfectly. Pests can munch their way happily from one plant to another, knowing that their young will have immediate access to their favourite food and generally making themselves at home as they start to build up their numbers. The simple act of mixing your crops with any kind of flower throws them into confusion. At the very least, they have to use up a little energy hunting for their food rather than just stumbling into it.

Put pests off the scent

Many pests find their favourite crops by smell. They will drift around fairly aimlessly until they get a whiff of, say, cabbage and then zero in on their prey. One of the simplest ways to confuse them, therefore, is by planting strong-smelling plants next to susceptible ones. Some of the most useful strong-smelling plants are those belonging to the allium (onion) family. Spring onions sown among carrots – either mixed in as part of the same row or in an adjacent row – may reduce attacks by the dreaded carrot fly, which tracks carrots down by the scent of their foliage and then lays its eggs in the soil near the carrot plants. It is also important to avoid crushing carrot foliage if possible, as this makes the smell stronger. When thinning, do not leave any bits of foliage lying around, and finish off by mounding up a little soil over the remaining carrots, as this provides a barrier that keeps the inevitable post-thinning visitors from getting to the roots.

If you are growing brassicas from seed (see chapter 10), alliums can also be used to ward off cabbage root fly. When you place a seed of your chosen brassica into the module of potting compost, drop one or two seeds of garlic chives (*Allium tuberosum*) in with it. The seeds will germinate at roughly the same time, and the smell of the garlic chives will mask the cabbage smell that the flies use for navigation, at a time when the brassica is at its most vulnerable. Alliums are also said to have beneficial antibacterial and antifungal properties, and so it may be worth mixing some in with any plants that are susceptible to rots.

Other particularly effective strong-smelling plants include French marigolds (*Tagetes patula*), which will throw aphids and whitefly off the scent of all sorts of plants, including tomatoes. Choose the varieties with the most pungent leaves and plant them all over your plot. All the strong-smelling herbs make great companion plants, particularly camomile (*Chamaemelum nobile*), feverfew (*Tanacetum parthenium*), lavender and thyme, and it is a good idea to plant a few of these throughout your plot at intervals, just to scent the air.

Good company

Another reason for companion planting is that sometimes plants can derive some benefit from each other's growth habit, and so grow more lustily in each other's company. A classic example is that of sweet corn, beans and squash. These were traditionally grown together by Native Americans because the squash covered the soil, suppressing weed growth and keeping it cool and moist, and the beans could use the sweet corn plants as support and climb up them. Potatoes and sweet corn also grow well together, as potatoes are good weed suppressors and, because of their differing habits, the plants do not compete for the same areas of soil and air. Lettuces grow well on the north side of tall plants such as runner beans, as they quickly go to flower in heat and so benefit from the shade. Again, the simple act of growing these plants in among each other, or in alternate rows

Beneficial insects

A popular use for companion planting is to bring in beneficial insects. These may pollinate crops, which will improve the yield on fruit plants and vegetables such as beans and marrows or, like hoverflies and lacewings, they may prey on garden pests. Different flowers attract different insects, so grow a range of companion plants if you can, to suit all tastes.

TO ATTRACT BEES
- Sage (*Salvia officinalis*)
- Marjoram (*Origanum vulgare*)
- Nasturtiums (*Tropaeolum majus*)
- Foxgloves (*Digitalis purpurea*)

TO ATTRACT BUTTERFLIES
- Sedums
- Mint (*Mentha* spp)
- Lavender (*Lavandula* spp)
- Sweet Williams (*Dianthus barbatus*)

TO ATTRACT PEST CONTROLLERS
- Cornflowers (*Centaurea cyanus*)
- Yarrow (*Achillea millefolium*)
- Coriander (*Coriandrum sativum*)
- Fennel (*Foeniculum vulgare*)
- Sweet alyssum (*Lobularia maritima*)

TO ATTRACT POLLINATORS
- Poached egg plants (*Limnanthes douglasii*)
- All kitchen herbs

rather than in large blocks, will lead to fewer pest problems.

Sacrificial plants

Sometimes companion plants can be used as sacrificial or lure plants to tempt pests away from edibles. Nasturtium (*Tropaeolum majus*) is an example. Grown close to any bean plant it will become

covered in blackfly that would otherwise swarm over the stems of the beans. Squash the blackfly on the plant with your hands, if you are not squeamish, or remove the worst-infested pieces of the plant and drop them into a soapy or salty solution to kill the pests.

PHYSICAL PROTECTION

Sometimes the simplest way of keeping pests off plants is to erect a physical barrier that they cannot get past. Horticultural fleece is often the best material for this. It is lightweight and so can be draped directly over plants, yet forms an impenetrable barrier. You may be concerned that it will stop light from getting to the plants, and so slow growth,

Fruit cages

If you have the time and money to set up a proper fruit cage, this will provide good protection from the attentions of birds at harvest time. A fruit cage is a large cage that is built over all your fruit trees and fruit bushes, and has a door in one side for you to gain access. It is covered in a mesh that will keep out birds but not pollinating insects. Fruit cages are better than draping the trees in fleece because they are permanent and easy to use once set up. This avoids the possibility of forgetting to cover the plants, or leaving it a little too late to do so. It also looks much better than mounds of fleece.

but in fact the light that gets through is reflected back off the lower surface of the fleece, and bounces on to the plants. It can even increase the amount of light the plants receive. Used in this way it can completely stop aphids, carrot fly, cabbage root fly and many other pests from getting at your plants.

It is also a good idea to consider fleece for the period when top and soft fruits start to ripen. They can be devastated by birds and wasps just as they are reaching their ripest and tastiest. Simply draping a large piece of fleece over your strawberry bed or apple tree and then pinning or tying it down will make it more difficult for these creatures to reach your precious crops. Fleece is usually best used as a temporary measure for keeping your fruit safe when pests are most active at the beginning of summer. This is because water may have some trouble penetrating it, or conversely, you may get a build-up of weeds and warm moist air underneath it, which will provide ideal conditions for moulds and rots to set in.

Brassicas suffer from the attentions of several pests, some of the worst of which are the cabbage white butterflies, which lay their eggs on the leaves. The eggs hatch and the caterpillars feed on the leaves. By erecting a structure of bamboo canes, hazel rods or wire hoops over the brassicas and covering this with a fine mesh you will keep the butterflies off and avoid the problem. A mesh will also exclude pigeons and other birds, which can occasionally attack brassicas. This may also suit other crops that might be attacked by birds, such as mange tout, sweet corn and soft fruits.

Cabbage root fly can be discouraged by companion planting and blocked by fleece, but a more conventional way is to use stem collars. Cabbage root fly lay their eggs at the base of the plant's stem, and the larvae then burrow down into the root. By placing a collar around the base of the plant – a 10cm (4in) disc of carpet underlay, roofing felt or cardboard with a slit cut in it – you stop the fly from getting access to the roots and so prevent the

Ants and aphid farming

If you notice that there are often ants around the aphids on your plants, it is likely that the ants are 'farming' the aphids. Aphids excrete honeydew, which contains undigested sugars, and this is useful food for ants. To protect their food source, ants will look after aphids, protecting them from predators and moving the fairly immobile pests around your plants to find more sappy and vulnerable parts.

problem from occurring. You can buy ready-made brassica collars from good garden centres.

Carrot fly can be confused by companion planting, but there is a complementary physical barrier that should keep them away from your carrots completely. Strange as it may sound, female carrot flies almost always travel low to the ground. This is their best position for smelling their quarry. When they reach a barrier that is 60cm (24in) high or taller, they will just fly around it. You can use this fact to your advantage by placing a board of this height, or some other impenetrable structure, around your carrots. This also works with pots; if you want to grow carrots in a container, choose one that is at least 60cm (24in) high and the carrot fly will not trouble them.

A sticky end

A rather unusual way to combat certain pests is to use a non-drying glue. This is most often used as a barrier to a pest of fruit called the winter moth, which attacks apples, pears, cherries and plums by laying its eggs near the buds in winter. In spring the larvae eat the buds, blossom and developing fruitlets. A band of non-drying glue or horticultural grease applied to the trunk in autumn will stop the females from crawling up the trunk to lay their eggs. The band should be applied about 1m (3ft) above soil level and be approximately 10cm (4in) wide. It can also be used to help stop ants farming aphids (see box on page 160): a barrier of non-drying glue applied around the trunk of a suitable affected plant should stop ants from travelling back

and forth to their charges. This will not wipe out your aphid infestation, but it will leave the aphids more vulnerable to predators.

Slugs and snails

Slugs and snails can be devastating, particularly early in the year, and they are among the hardest pests to control well. Slug pellets are effective, but they may be harmful to other creatures that might eat them, and to those, such as hedgehogs, that might eat slugs that have eaten them. If applied precisely as per the manufacturer's directions – in other words sprinkled evenly but very thinly – they are relatively harmless. Biological controls can be very effective against slugs, but not snails (see page 168).

You may find that barrier methods work. It is certainly a good idea to try every available method against them, as no method works alone. Try covering young plants completely with small cloches, such

as a plastic bottle that has had the base cut out of it and is pushed down into the earth to prevent slugs from reaching the plant. This can be effective, but the plant will soon outgrow the space available and the mini cloche will have to be removed if it is not to be detrimental to the plant. Another method is to place a ring around the plant made of something slugs and snails are reluctant to cross. This could be a sharp material, such as gravel or cockleshells, or it could be a mat or a ring made of copper, which gives off a slight electrical charge that slugs and snails are supposed to dislike. There are also products based on

wool fibres that the pests are said to find irritating. However, the barrier method can be fiddly and is also of questionable efficacy; sometimes, particularly in wet weather, slime trails will show that the slugs have simply clambered over your sharpest weaponry.

OPPOSITE A cut-down plastic bottle provides an effective barrier against slugs, but plants soon outgrow the space available.
ABOVE Copper rings are said to drive slugs and snails away by giving off an electrical discharge, but sometimes these pests will cross any barrier.

Beer traps

Another method that is worth trying with slugs is a beer trap. This involves placing a small receptacle of beer near vulnerable plants. Slugs are attracted to the smell of the beer, crawl in and drown. You need to cover the beer trap so that the beer is not watered down with rainwater. Make sure that the opening is high up enough that other creatures do not drop in, and the slugs have to actively crawl in. An old plastic milk container with a small amount of beer in the bottom buried into the ground a few centimetres (1in), with a hole cut about 5cm (2in) above the surface of the soil, makes an ideal trap. Alternatively you can buy ready-made traps. This method does collect plenty of slug bodies, but it is pretty gruesome.

You could also try scattering cut leaves of lettuce or weed seedlings near your plants. Slugs are supposed to prefer wilting vegetation to that which is actively growing, so the idea is that they fill themselves up on your wilted offerings and leave your plants alone. Obviously this has the disadvantage that you are actively feeding them up and so are encouraging a growth in the slug population, which could come back to haunt you when you forget to put out any cut leaves. It is worth trying in addition to other methods, however.

TIMING

Sometimes it is possible to avoid pests by sowing seeds at specific times of year. One example is broad beans. They almost always become completely covered in

blackfly in spring. This is particularly a problem if you have sown them in early spring, because the top growth is soft and sappy and therefore more vulnerable to attack. However, by sowing suitable cultivars in late autumn or winter, the seeds germinate early and then toughen up over winter. They get a head start in spring, and have often flowered by the time the worst of the blackfly attacks begin. They also have tougher, less susceptible growth. If the plants have flowered before the blackfly starts to attack, it is much easier to control the pest. Blackfly always colonize the growing point of the plant, and you can pinch this out without affecting the flowers or developing bean pods.

Timing is also important in carrot growing. Carrot flies only lay eggs at certain times of the year, and so by timing

OPPOSITE Beer traps can prove very effective, but emptying out the drowned and decaying slug bodies can be quite a gruesome task.
ABOVE Horticultural fleece is a very lightweight material that can be draped directly over plants without doing too much damage.

your sowings you can make sure that no carrots are at a vulnerable stage at those times. Unprotected sowings can be carried out from late winter to mid-spring, from early to mid-summer and from early to mid-autumn. You can still make sowings at other times, but if you do, use one of the protection methods given above, or cover the whole bed in fleece until the seedlings are at a less vulnerable stage.

BIOLOGICAL CONTROL

The development of biological controls that you can buy and apply to your allotment is fantastic for the half-hour allotmenteer. These controls are entirely natural and organic, and are safe to use around wildlife, pets or children. Their application generally just involves watering or sprinkling a pre-prepared pack of nematodes or other creatures on to the soil or directly on to the affected plants. In return you get several weeks of control (at the very least) without having to do anything else. They are expensive, but if you are prepared to spend the money they can be extremely effective.

Slug nematodes

One of the best-known biological controls is for slugs. A nematode that preys on slugs occurs naturally in the soil, but not in the sort of numbers required to keep them under control and prevent them from making a mess of your plants. These nematodes can be bought commercially in the form of a powdered product which you add to water and then sprinkle over the soil, so boosting numbers. You will need to make several applications to keep the slug population down throughout the growing season, but the control is extremely effective. It can be applied from early spring until mid-autumn outdoors, or at any time of the year under glass. It is a good idea to start early, especially if you are planting out young, tender seedlings, of which slugs are particularly fond. As it is a naturally occurring slug predator it does no harm to

ABOVE Slug nematodes are watered directly on to the soil. Follow with an application of fresh water to wash any nematode solution off the leaves.

any other wildlife, even those that might eat the dying slugs after they have been infected with the nematodes.

Lacewings and ladybirds

The larvae of lacewings and ladybirds are fantastic at controlling aphids. You can try to attract them by using companion planting (see page 156), but if you still suffer from high populations of aphids, it is possible to buy in reinforcements. Lacewings are bought as larvae and sprinkled directly on to affected plants. These larvae munch through the aphids, before turning into adults. These adults then lay more eggs, often among aphid

colonies, which will emerge as carnivorous larvae. Both ladybird adults and larvae eat lots of aphids. They can be bought as larvae and, again, sprinkled directly on to affected plants. Adult ladybirds will lay eggs and the larvae hatch out and help with control. Many suppliers sell ladybird and lacewing houses or boxes, but as there is no shortage of naturally occurring overwintering sites for these insects, such purchases may not be necessary.

Control under cover

It is in polytunnels and greenhouses, where pests can thrive in the warm conditions, that biological controls work best, as the enclosed environment means that the predators and parasites are less likely to wander elsewhere. The two most common problems are glasshouse whitefly and glasshouse red spider mite. The former is controlled by a parasitic wasp, *Encarsia formosa*, which lays its eggs in the whitefly's scale-like nymphs. Red spider mite is controlled by a predatory mite, *Phytoseiulus persimilis*. These and other biological controls can be ordered through some garden centres or from mail order suppliers.

Homes for helpers

Sometimes you cannot buy the helpful creatures themselves, you can buy homes that they will find and colonize. Native bees are worth mentioning here, even though they are not needed to keep down pests or diseases. A high population of native bees will improve the quality and quantity of your crops, simply because they are fantastic pollinators. Pollination issues are frustrating for gardeners, as unpollinated fruit will often look as if it has set and is going to develop into delicious fruit, only to drop off the tree later on. Red mason bees fly and feed early in the year from early spring to mid-summer, and so are handy for pollinating tree fruit such as apples, pears and plums, and soft fruit such as strawberries, which flower at these times. Blue mason bees fly and feed from late spring to early autumn, and so are more useful for those vegetables that require pollination for a good crop, such as beans and marrows.

Different-sized homes are available for each type of bee. The homes are bundles of small hollow tubes into which the bees crawl and lay their eggs before sealing them off. In autumn, you should remove the home from the allotment and store it in a cool, frost-free place until the following spring, when it can be brought out again and re-hung, preferably near the crop you are hoping to pollinate. Bumblebees are good all-round pollinators, and homes are also available for these.

Hedgehogs and slow worms are also useful creatures to have about, mainly because of their love of slugs. You can buy smart hedgehog homes, in which hedgehogs can hibernate over winter, or you can create a dry and cosy home out of logs. Logs also provide a habitat for slow worms and many other creatures. If you

have no access to logs, one of the best slow worm shelters is a piece of corrugated iron, left on the ground.

SPRAYING

There are some problems that can only be controlled by spraying. Potato and tomato blight are tricky to control, and are often worth treating pre-emptively. Copper oxychloride and Bordeaux mixture can be sprayed before there is any sign of attack. These fungicides are considered suitable for use in organic systems and can also be used to treat other fungal problems. Sulphur dust is also considered suitable for organic gardeners and can be used to control powdery mildew. Take care to follow instructions on timing, application rates and the length of time between spraying and harvesting when using garden sprays. Even though they are organic, sprays are not good enough to eat.

Plants fight back

Sometimes you can use plants themselves to solve their own problems. Onion leaves can be used in the fight against white rot, a fungal disease of alliums. Once white rot spores have infected a plant, the will lie in the ground for years until another allium is planted, and then leap into action. It can take at least ten years of not growing alliums in that area for the spores to die. However, if you chop up some onion leaves and dig them into the soil of the affected area, the spores will migrate onto them and go to work. The leaves, not being attached to a living plant, soon die, and the spores with them.

OPPOSITE Luxury accommodation: a bee hotel provides nesting and hibernation spots for a wide variety of useful pollinating insects.

A wildlife garden

If you are creating an organic allotment, that is a good reason for having an area that is left a little rough and ready, in which wildlife can thrive. However, there is always loads of wildlife on all allotments, whether you actively encourage it or not – wildlife is attracted to green spaces – and there are several drawbacks to giving over a whole area to wildlife that you should keep in mind.

The first is that wildlife areas are messy. This is an important consideration if you are trying to keep your plot going with the minimum of time and fuss. Grass and weeds left to grow turn to seed, which can spread all over your own plot and your neighbours'. Slugs and snails can hide in long grass and emerge at night to eat vulnerable seedlings. The fact that wildlife areas usually don't look great will seem to real nature lovers to be a side issue, but it can make life harder if you are trying to keep on top of a plot and on an allotment site you may have to get used to sly comments from your neighbours. If your fellow gardeners are not organically minded, a wildlife area could easily be construed as a neglected area, and this could get you a warning or a threat of eviction.

Friendly features

It may be simpler and less time consuming just to put in a few wildlife friendly features, rather than giving over a whole area to wildlife. These could include a small pond, for frogs, and a couple of insect houses. If you do decide to create a wildlife garden on your plot, mow around the perimeter of it regularly and surround it with an edging of sharp gravel. This will make it look smarter and 'deliberate', and it should also help contain the slugs and snails.

RIGHT Don't worry too much if your wildlife area looks a little messy.
OPPOSITE Much of the wildlife attracted to your plot will be useful, like pest-eating birds (top left), hoverflies (top right) and hedgehogs (bottom left) – but be prepared for a few less helpful visitors such as mice (bottom right).

AN ALLOTMENT FOR CHILDREN

There are many good reasons for making allotments into places where children — if you have them — can spend time. The first is purely practical. You need to put time in if you are to look after your plot properly, and if you have children to look after as well, you need to find something for them to do while you are on the allotment. If they love visiting it too they will be happy to tag along and will be much less likely to make a fuss about wanting to go home to watch telly just ten minutes after you have arrived. You will also avoid getting into complex childcare arrangements every time you want to pop up to the plot for half an hour. However, very young children, no matter how much they like being on the allotment, may require more supervision than you can properly give them while working on your plot. It pays to be realistic from the outset.

OUTDOOR EDUCATION

Beyond such practicalities, there are perhaps more worthy reasons for taking children to the allotment. There can be few better all-round educational activities than gardening. Many children grow up having no idea where a pea or a tomato actually comes from, and this gap in knowledge prevents them appreciating the difference between good, fresh food and junk. Creating a sense of wonder at growing and harvesting food at an early age will help to set them up for a lifetime of healthy eating. If they have grown a crop themselves, nurturing it from seed to harvest, they are much more likely to want to at least try eating it than if it is all ready prepared for them and plonked on a plate.

Many parents use small pets such as hamsters or goldfish to teach their children about responsibility and nurturing, but this can be a bit of a gamble. Small children, or those with particularly short attention spans, can quickly get bored, and the choice to the parent quickly becomes whether to take on the pet care for themselves or leave the poor little thing to suffer. Usually, the parent steps in and the children only learn that mum will bail them out if they can't be bothered to do something. Gardening, on the other hand, introduces children to a gentle discipline without the heavy responsibility of the fate of a small mammal resting in their hands. Most parents will be able to cope with a couple of tomato plants dying, whereas they would feel the need to intervene with a starved and desperate gerbil. The child with plants to care for learns cause and effect: care for it and it lives; neglect it and it dies. Not a bad lesson to take on early in life.

On a more academic note, there are many opportunities for teaching a bit of basic science up the allotment. Pollination, germination, changing seasons, ripening fruits: the curious child will see all these happening around them and will want to know why and how. Most of us, no matter how non-academic our backgrounds, are up to explaining the basics, and it might even make certain conversations a little less painful if they already understand what that bee is doing to that apple blossom.

GETTING CHILDREN INVOLVED

Children are territorial creatures and will relish the opportunity of caring for their own patch of ground, so give them their own area to look after. Particularly if they share a room with a sibling, or if they have no other access to a garden, a space of their own will be a matter of great pride and enjoyment; a place where they can really express themselves without their little brother or big sister cramping their style. If you have more than one child, don't be mean and make them share but give them an area each, even if that means giving them less space.

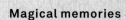

Magical memories

Anyone who spent any amount of time in a garden in their childhood will remember it as a magical place of play and discovery. A child will look back on quality time spent with you on your allotment with great pleasure and nostalgia for the rest of their lives, no matter how hard it was in reality to actually get them up there.

In fact, a child's plot needs to be fairly small in order to be manageable. A square 2m (6ft) by 1.2m (4ft), or a strip 2.5m (8ft) by 0.6m (2ft), should be more than enough for starters. Giving them an unworkable burden would be counter-productive, and could put them off gardening for life.

You might consider delineating their area by making it into a raised bed. This would involve digging the area over and removing all traces of weeds, before lining the edges of the bed with planks of wood or similar, and then filling in with topsoil, garden compost, manure and possibly grit and sand, if the soil is heavy. The idea is that all the really tough work that might put them off is done for them before they start, in order to set them off on an optimistic foot. It may seem expensive to buy in a load of topsoil but it will be a worthwhile investment. You want to make it incredibly easy for them to succeed, at least at first, and by the time you are ready for them to get going, the soil should be the best you have on the plot.

LEFT Get children interested in gardening by growing the things they like to eat. A supersize strawberry will always go down well.

WHAT TO GROW

What they grow will depend to a certain extent on what they eat. If they have favourite vegetables it is definitely worth including them, but there are also some plants that are sure-fire winners with most kids. Radishes are great, simply because they germinate and grow so fast, but unfortunately they are a little too peppery for most children's tastes. Carrots are probably the next best things in terms of the speed with which they develop into edible plants, and their sweet taste, especially when young, makes them a favourite. Encourage your child to sow them close together and then to thin them as they grow, eating the sweet, tender thinnings immediately. Tomatoes are good, especially the small, sweet, cherry varieties such as 'Sweet 100' that they can pop into their mouths the moment they are ripe, although tomatoes will take a little more patience and dedication than carrots. New potatoes may not seem an obvious choice, but in fact children love the process of digging them up and discovering the buried treasure under the ground. You can then continue their food education by taking the potatoes home to boil, blob with butter and eat that night. Big and bold plants will always hold a special place in the hearts of children, most of whom love to win above all else. Giant pumpkin and sunflower competitions will spur them on to take the best possible care of their charges, even if organized just between family and friends, but particularly if they culminate in a public event where they can really show off their hard work, such as an allotment show.

For outsized pumpkins give them seeds of 'Atlantic Giant' and for the tallest possible sunflowers go for 'Giant Single'.

TRY BRIBERY

There are other ways of harnessing children's competitive instincts at the allotment. I recently saw an allotment neighbour with a couch-grass infested area to clear; this patch was cleared within ten minutes by offering the three children in her charge 'a penny a root'. Particularly big roots qualified for twice or even 3 times this rate (to discourage sly chopping up of big ones) and an extra incentive was offered to the child who gathered the most. The kids had soon gathered a mound of roots each. She had kept them occupied while she finished her work, and had a weed-free patch of land for a small outlay, while they went away chuffed that they had made a bit of extra money. The key to the success of this kind of bribery and corruption is not to push your luck. Allotting a fairly short amount of time (say ten minutes) and restricting the area to be cleared (perhaps a square metre/yard or two each) will help them believe that it is a real competition and not a dastardly parental trick to get them to do the backbreaking work for peanuts. Plan ahead and have the money to hand to help suspend any suspicions that they are being taken for a ride.

KEEP THEM SAFE

Create areas of your plot where children can just hang out and play safely. Allotments are not places where you want

Children's favourites

These are a few varieties are especially suitable for children to grow.

- Carrot 'Parmex': bite-sized round, sweet roots
- Courgette 'Floridor': bright yellow, perfectly round fruits like tennis balls
- Radish 'Rainbow Mixed': a kaleidoscope of purple, white, golden and red radishes
- Salad leaves 'Niche': a good mix of different leaf shapes, colours, textures and flavours
- Salad onion 'Apache': mild flavoured with a purple skin
- Squash 'Sunburst': golden, scalloped fruits like flying saucers
- Sunflower 'Teddy Bear': only 15cm (6in) tall but bears huge, fluffy, ridiculously double yellow flowers
- Tomato 'Berry': unusual, strawberry-shaped, cherry-sized fruits with a sweet flavour

OPPOSITE Carrots are quick to grow and children will love discovering "buried treasure" as they pull the roots from the soil.

kids to run wild. There are bamboo canes sticking out of the ground and bits of glass and rusting metal hanging around under long grass that they could hurt themselves on. Not all allotment gardeners are child friendly either, and you may end up getting complaints if your little darlings are too excitable and on too loose a rein. If you have grassed over part of your plot while you work on making a smaller area usable, this spare area can make a perfect child-friendly spot. Create fun features such as a willow stem den. Just push pieces of willow into the ground and bend them over and tie them together to create corridors or play houses. Once pushed into the ground the

stems take root, and the entire structure is soon covered in fresh, green leaves, providing privacy for young adventurers. Slides, covered sandpits, climbing frames and swings would be good additions to this sort of area, as would self-contained games such as swingball, but remember to check for allotment restrictions before you start. Normal ball games should certainly be discouraged as they can wreak havoc on sheds, plants, ripe produce and neighbourly relations. The long handles of rakes and spades are also positively hazardous – to other children nearby, as well as adults, plants and shed windows. Children will find normal size tools heavy and unwieldy to use and there is every possibility that they might hurt themselves with them. A set of sturdy, colourful, child-sized tools will be safer as well as easier for them to use.

STRUCTURING CHILDREN'S TIME

You may find that once children have caught the bug, they do not need this sort of distraction or too much supervision and are happy to work away under their own steam. Children have short attention spans, however, and it can be worth creating a gardening timetable that

panders to this. You can easily adapt the half-hour system to suit them – perhaps create a quarter-hour system. Children will get bored of any dull jobs within a few minutes, but they should learn that weeding and digging are essential parts of the gardening process.

Bearing this in mind, break up their quarter hour into three five-minute slots, each five minutes to be spent on a different job. So one day's work might include five minutes each of watering, weeding and preparing a bed for seed sowing. The next day might be earthing up potatoes, watering and sowing seeds. Just as with your own time, the pattern of jobs will change with the seasons. If you can make each job well defined in terms of the time allotted, your child will see gardening as a series of small, achievable tasks rather than an endless battle with no end in sight.

A practical way to enforce this is to buy each child a simple wind-up egg timer, which they or you can set as they start each job to go off after five minutes. This way they can easily measure the time for themselves. Once they have finished their fifteen minutes' work, don't forget to shower them with praise before they can have free time to play, or to help you out.

WHAT NEXT?

This book has, I hope, given you the tools you need to create an allotment that you can manage in tandem with a busy life, rather than one that you have to devote half your life to. If you follow its advice, you should have an allotment that produces a supply of seasonal fresh vegetables all year round, all for just half an hour's work a day. But some people really get the bug and start wanting to develop their allotmenting skills. This final chapter is designed to give you ideas on where to go next, if you feel you have the energy and the time to do more. I want to recommend some things that keep you within the basic tenet of the half-hour system: they should either increase the quality of the crops you produce or the ease with which you can produce them.

RAISING YOUR OWN PLANTS FROM SEED

One way in which you might want to branch out on your allotment is in trying out some unusual cultivars. One of the methods this book has suggested to make your life easier is to use the services of plug plant nurseries to buy in small seedlings of certain vegetable plants, where this proves simpler than direct sowing. However, the number and variety of cultivars that are available in the form of plug plants is very limited, and you may find that after a few years you long to experiment with some new, unusual or heritage cultivars; perhaps some new varieties that have been bred for resistance to particular diseases or pests that are prevalent on your plot.

To find 'different' seeds, start to look out for seed catalogues from smaller or specialist companies, and talk to fellow allotment holders about the sources of their seeds. Look in the back of gardening magazines, or on the internet, for nurseries that sell unusual ranges of seed, and send off for their catalogues to see if there is anything that appeals to you. Smaller nurseries are often run by real enthusiasts, and you will find it hard to resist their descriptions.

Starting from scratch

If you decide you want to try experimenting with some of these new and different cultivars, you will have to start sowing your own, rather than buying seedlings in.

The usual way is to start off by sowing your seeds into seed trays, and leaving them to germinate on your windowsill. Once they germinate, you prick them out, lifting the individual seedlings by their leaves out of the soil and quickly transferring them into a small pot or module of soil. You then place them back on the windowsill while they grow a bit larger. For a slightly simpler way of doing things, forget this whole pricking-out business and sow single seeds straight into your final container, be that pot or module. The drawback to this is that not all will germinate, and so you will have some waste of compost or pots for those that do not. Weigh this small amount of waste up

against the palaver of the whole pricking-out business, though, and you will see that it is worth a few empty modules or pots.

Trays of different-sized modules can be bought at garden centres, and these are particularly useful as they hold only a small amount of soil, so there is less chance of a small seedling getting waterlogged than there would be in a pot. However, they will only really be suitable for small seedlings, and certainly not for larger ones such as courgettes or tomatoes, which must go straight into a pot.

Some seeds will seem so small that you may find it impossible to sow one per module. This is not a problem: you can sow a few to a pot and then pull out the weaker seedlings at a later date. This can seem wasteful, but remember that every seed packet is likely to contain enough potential vegetables to serve several families, and so a few lost plants at this stage is not the end of the world. Use the chart in chapter 4 to see how many plants you really need. Sow a few more than this to allow for losses, but don't be tempted to sow the whole packet simply because they are there.

Under cover

If you have a greenhouse or polytunnel (see page 194), this is the ideal place to sow these seeds, to keep them out of the house. But most people, particularly those who are new to gardening or short

Heritage cultivars

These are old, long-established varieties that have disappeared from seed catalogues in favour of different or more fashionable cultivars. Many heritage cultivars have a reputation for doing well under certain difficult circumstances, perhaps similar to your own, and they are often renowned for having a particularly good taste. Seeds may not be available to buy, because of European legislation that requires all seed for sale to be included on a national or EU list, but they can be sourced through special libraries, such as the Heritage Seed Library (www.gardenorganic.org.uk)

OPPOSITE TOP Purple-podded peas are an unusual sight but very practical – they stand out against the green foliage, making them easy to pick.
OPPOSITE BOTTOM Heritage tomato varieties may be oddly shaped but they often have a truly magnificent flavour.

on space at home, will not have one. Instead of hopelessly lusting after one, invest in a temporary plastic greenhouse.

These are usually made of a metal, foldable frame around which is hung a clear plastic covering. This can be zipped up at night to keep the cold out, or unzipped for easy access or to allow ventilation on warmer days. They provide enough protection and let in enough light for your seedlings to thrive, but are usually extremely compact and can fit into even the smallest back garden.

The real beauty of these temporary structures is that they can be folded up and put away in the loft or the shed as soon as they are no longer in use, once you've put the plants out on to the allotment. A drawback is that they are not as insulated as greenhouses and so plants inside them are more vulnerable to frost. You may have to cover them with a blanket or a layer of bubble wrap on particularly cold spring nights.

A compact alternative to temporary greenhouses is a cold frame. These low boxes with glass lids can be utilized in the same way. They are more permanent, though, as they are often made from wood and glass and are therefore heavy and cumbersome to move out of the way after you have planted out your seedlings.

Hardening off

With all seedlings that you grow yourself, there will need to be a period of hardening off to prevent them from getting too much of a shock when they are first planted out. For seedlings and young plants you have raised in your home, as the weather starts to warm up in spring, start moving them outside during the day to harden them off, but bring them in at night in case of late frosts. You want to put them outside enough to give them plenty of light to avoid them becoming drawn-up and leggy, but you must be careful not to leave them out during weather that is too cold for them.

If your young plants are in a temporary greenhouse, start off by opening the zips of the greenhouse during warm days, always closing them again at night. Move on to fully opening up the greenhouse in the day and closing it at night, and eventually, near planting out time, and when you know that the danger of frost has passed, leave it open all the time.

The last frost date for your area will be anywhere between early spring and early summer, depending on a number of factors, including how built up your area is, and its latitude, altitude and proximity to the sea. Even if you can make a rough guess at the

last frost date, every year will be different, and there is always a danger of a sneaky late frost, so remember to check the local weather forecasts regularly, and to close up the greenhouse if frost is forecast. It is better to be safe than to lose a whole load of seedlings in one night.

STORING PRODUCE

Storage has hardly been touched upon in this book, and with good reason – you should always aim to harvest fresh and eat immediately. This is the way to enjoy your crops when they are at their best.

However, there will be times when you have more of a certain crop than you can eat immediately. This is particularly the case with fruit trees and bushes, the fruit of which has a tendency to all ripen at around the same time.

Some crops can be stored simply over autumn and winter in a frost-free shed, including root crops such as carrots and celeriac, and tree fruit such as apples and pears. Paper or fabric sacks and sturdy cardboard boxes will be useful for these.

ABOVE A cold frame is a good way of achieving some extra-early crops. It is also a very useful place to harden off seedlings and young plants.

Freezing

Try to avoid freezing as far as possible. Unless you have a large chest freezer or two, you will soon run out of space you need for other purposes such as ice cream. The process is generally detrimental to the quality of the produce, which takes on a mushy consistency no matter how fresh and crisp it started off.

If you must freeze, do so as soon as possible after harvesting. Wash the fruits or vegetables thoroughly, discarding any that are not at their best, and trim and cut into serving-sized pieces, as necessary. Vegetables will need to be blanched or briefly steamed and then cooled quickly in icy water before freezing. This step inactivates enzymes that will damage flavour, nutrients and texture during freezer storage. After preparation, spread the fruit or vegetables out on a tray covered in baking parchment so that they are not touching, and put the whole lot in the freezer. Once they have frozen, you can bundle them all into a freezer bag or box and pop them back into the freezer. This means that they will not all be stuck together in a big lump when you come to use them, and can be used in small quantities if necessary.

Bottling

Bottling is a far more interesting alternative to freezing. When you bottle fruits you have to combine them with syrup or fruit juice, and this process alone can make the crop into a higher-quality product. You can also make your crops into ready-to-use sauces such

ABOVE Bottled fruit in syrup provides you with ready-made pie fillings or sauces and will keep well for up to a year.

as fruit pie fillings or pasta sauce and bottle those.

You will need to buy some special bottling jars and lids. Sterilize jars, bottles and lids in boiling water and then air-dry before filling with the prepared fruit or sauce. Cover fruit with syrup (made by boiling two parts sugar and eight parts water together until the sugar is dissolved) or fruit juice. Replace the lids and then put the jars into a large saucepan of water. They should be kept off the base of the saucepan using a wire rack, so that they do not get too hot and crack.

Boil for about thirty minutes: this heat processing creates a sterile, vacuum-sealed environment inside the container. Remove the jars (you can buy special tongs for this purpose) and leave to cool overnight. You will know that the jars are sealed if the lids have a slight depression and do not move when touched; if a vacuum seal does not result from heat processing, refrigerate the product and use within one week. Make sure that you label everything well, store somewhere dark and cool and use within the year. Discard any preserves that have deteriorated or have damaged or swollen seals.

Home-made preserves

Of course you can also make all sorts of jams, chutneys and pickles as a way of

Bottling tomatoes

Bottling produce that is low in acid, which means most vegetables, can lead to a risk of botulism poisoning, and so is not recommended for home bottlers. The one exception is tomatoes, which are botanically a fruit and contain sufficient acid to be safe; even so, many recipes recommend the addition of lemon juice. Skin the tomatoes by plunging them into boiling water for a minute and then directly into cold water, when the skins should slip off easily. Quarter or chop them and pack them into the jars, then either cover them with brine or pack them down well and leave them to form their own juice.

using up excess produce and turning your crops into a high-quality product that is easy to store. There are lots of different recipes available in dozens of books or on the internet.

Preserves rely on the preservative effects of sugar for jams and jellies, or vinegar for pickles, or a combination of the two for chutneys. For jams, fruit should be under-ripe rather than over-ripe, as jam made from over-ripe fruit does not set well. Use your over-ripe fruit, combined with a variety of surplus vegetables, to make a delicious and unique allotment chutney.

Drying

Another interesting way of storing excess crops is to dry them. In hot countries with a predictable climate this is done out of doors in the sun. Sun-dried tomatoes and peppers have almost all the moisture evaporated out of them, which intensifies the flavours, and they can be stored for long periods. In countries that might not have the luxury of long runs of good weather there are other ways of drying foods. If you have a warm conservatory or a particularly warm area of your house, you can just hang bunches of your chosen produce up to dry naturally. This is especially effective if you have a stove or a heater that gives out constant heat.

You can also prepare fruit and vegetables on baking trays by slicing them and removing any seeds or leaving as they are, before placing them in an oven at its lowest heat overnight, and with the door propped open to let out the evaporating moisture. The larger the pieces, the longer they will take to dry.

If all this sounds like too much fuss, though, you can buy an Italian-style drying machine, which comprises a number of racks on which to place your prepared vegetables. The machine removes excess moisture and you are left with a 'sun-dried' product that can be stored in sterilized jars, either dry or topped up with oil.

Drying is suitable for herbs, tomatoes, peppers and chillies, as well as for fruits such as apricots and apples, and you can experiment with all sorts of crops to see how well they dry.

POLYTUNNELS

After a couple of years on your allotment, you are quite likely to start hankering after a polytunnel – a metal frame with a skin of plastic stretched over it. I prefer polytunnels to greenhouses, with good reason. Greenhouses are less suitable for the allotment. They are more expensive, they can be magnets for vandals, and panes of glass are easily broken. A polytunnel is cheaper and will do the job just as well.

Polytunnels extend the seasons in which you can grow certain crops, and they improve the quality of the crops that you are already producing. At the beginning of the year you will be able to plant out your more tender vegetables such as melons, courgettes, peppers and aubergines weeks before you could outside, and without the danger of them being affected by frost. This will mean that they will start cropping earlier in the year. You can use a polytunnel as a space for bringing on seedlings, should you decide that you want to, and so avoid the need to erect even a temporary home greenhouse. In this sense polytunnels can be particularly useful for those who lack garden space at home.

At the end of the summer, you can use a polytunnel to ripen fruits that need a long season: you will end up with far fewer green tomatoes to dispose of if you grow tomatoes under a polytunnel. Over winter, a polytunnel provides a place that is sufficiently sheltered for many things to be able to keep growing more strongly than they would out of doors, allowing you to continue to crop young, tender lettuce leaves and carrots throughout the coldest months.

A final reason for having a polytunnel is that it is handy to have somewhere on your plot that is always warm and dry, and where you have control over the elements. It is a great place for curing vegetables such as pumpkins and garlic, which need a warm, dry spell and good ventilation if they are to store well. A polytunnel also allows you to spend time at the allotment during the wettest weather.

What to buy?

Before you buy, check your allotment site's rules; some have height or other restrictions that would forbid the erection of a polytunnel, or limit the size you go for. Otherwise, the larger the polytunnel, the better; you will find that you soon fill it up.

Be aware, too, that you will need to manage your polytunnel, and having one will add to the list of jobs you have to do regularly. For instance, in winter the doors will be permanently shut, but there will be times in late spring when you may need to open the doors in the morning and return to close them up at night, so as to keep the temperature relatively stable.

Setting up

It is important that you clear the site well before you erect a polytunnel. Once it is up, it will provide a warm and often humid environment – perfect growing conditions for most plants, including weeds. Treat the soil of the polytunnel area as thoroughly as you would a new piece of ground that you were about to start planting up, if not more so.

When setting the polytunnel up, it is a good idea to lay a path up its centre. This could be made from paving stones, gravel, woodchips or even grass. A table at about waist height can be extremely useful in a polytunnel. It can be a propagating bench in spring, or you can use it as extra growing space when you run out. You may also want to use it to raise seedlings up off the ground to keep them away from slugs.

Although plants can be planted straight into the soil inside a polytunnel, it might be a good idea to use growing bags or large pots of soil instead. The space within a polytunnel is pretty limited, so you do not have the space to put a real system of rotation into place. If you grow tomatoes in the same spot in the polytunnel year after year, you will get a build-up of tomato pests and diseases in the soil. Pots and growing bags will give you more watering work but will be worth it in the long run.

Watering and ventilation

Since you are cutting plants off from any natural source of water and making them entirely dependent on you, you must take great care over watering in a polytunnel. Water regularly, and water into the soil,

ABOVE A firm path up the centre of a polytunnel will allow easy access and keep your feet clean and dry. Paving slabs are ideal.
OPPOSITE A polytunnel is the perfect place to grow early salad crops. Choose the right varieties and you could have lettuce all through the winter.

rather than on to the leaves. Polytunnels can get extremely humid, and damp leaves in a humid environment can lead to rots setting in.

High humidity is the main reason why ventilation of polytunnels is so important. Try to buy a tunnel that has openings at each end, to allow for a complete exchange of air. Ventilation will be most important at the height of summer, when polytunnels can really overheat and cause plants to wilt, but it will be necessary in warm spells during other seasons too.

GROWING AND SHOWING

The time will come when you feel so confident of the crops you are producing that you are ready to try your luck at the local flower show or allotment fair. You are most likely to measure your success by how often you have fresh, delicious, tender vegetables on your dinner plate, rather than by their size, but there is still a place for you at the fair. Times have changed, and growing the longest leek or the largest pumpkin is no longer considered the pinnacle of success. At the least a flower show or fair is an opportunity to meet fellow gardeners and to have a bit of fun; it can also be a chance to show off your achievements.

What the judges are looking for

It is true that in some places you will still find a group of old boys competing fiercely to produce the straightest runner bean, but on most sites you will be surprised at how well your produce measures up, and it is always worth having a go. You do not need to have been paying your chosen vegetable constant attention or feeding it with a specially formulated fertilizer. The most important criterion for the judging of vegetables in allotment shows is actually not size at all but uniformity. If it is the height of summer and your produce is ripening daily, you should have plenty to choose from.

The most important thing to remember for all shows is to read the schedule properly and make sure your entry complies. There are few things worse than seeing your splendid specimen disqualified as 'NAS' – not according to schedule.

Flavour comes first

Your secret weapon, however, will be flavour. In many allotment shows the judges will not just look at the produce but taste it too. If you have made it your mission to produce only the tastiest, most tender vegetables for your own table, the judges will appreciate this, especially if they compare them with larger but tougher or more watery offerings. You will have an extra advantage if you have started to use more unusual or heritage cultivars, as these will provide different flavours from those of your competitors and make your produce stand out.

There will also usually be awards given for products made from allotment produce. If you have made any pickles, dried or bottled fruits or jams, this is the place to get them out and have them judged. Again, presentation is important, and your jars should be tidy and neatly labelled, but it is taste that will win the day.

With a bit of luck you will come away with a clutch of certificates, but at the very least you will have a lot of fun and have a chance to swap tips with fellow allotmenteers on coping with your specific conditions and the best cultivars. And if you do win a few prizes, it will be confirmation that allotments are all about the eating, and that you are eating the very best.

OPPOSITE Local shows give you the chance to show off your best produce. Even if you don't win a prize you can have fun trying!

WHAT NEXT?

Some mail order suppliers

You may be lucky enough to have an excellent garden centre or nursery near to your allotment where you can buy a good range of plants and seeds, as well as many of the other sundry items you need for your plot. However, few garden centres are likely to have a wide enough choice of fruit and vegetable plants and seeds to satisfy you once you get started, and this is where specialist mail order suppliers will come to your rescue. Listed below are a few of the major players, but keep an eye out for addresses of new or more specialist, smaller outfits in gardening magazines, or ask around your allotment neighbours for their recommendations. When ordering for deliveries by post, remember to get your order in early, so that plants can be delivered on time.

SEED AND VEGETABLE PLANT SUPPLIERS:

Chiltern Seeds Limited
Crowmarsh Battle Barns, 114 Preston
Crowmarsh, Wallingford, OX10 6SL
Tel: 01491 824675
www.chilternseeds.co.uk
Suppliers of a very interesting selection
of vegetable and herb seeds

Delfland Nurseries Ltd
Benwick Road, Doddington, March,
Cambridgeshire, PE15 0TU
Tel: 01354 740553
Fax: 01354 741200
www.organicplants.co.uk
Suppliers of organic vegetable plants

Dobies of Devon
Long Road, Paignton, Devon, TQ4 7SX
Tel: 0844 701 7625
www.dobies.co.uk
Suppliers of a wide range of vegetables,
flowers and herbs

Johnsons Seeds
Gazeley Road, Kentford, Suffolk, CB8 7QB
Tel: 0845 6589147
www.johnsons-seeds.com
Suppliers of a wide range of vegetables,
flowers and herbs

Marshalls Seeds
Alconbury Hill, Huntingdon,
Cambridgeshire, PE28 4HY
Tel: 0844 557 6700
www.marshalls-seeds.co.uk
Suppliers of a wide range of vegetables,
flowers and herbs

Mr Fothergills Seeds
Gazeley Road, Kentford, Suffolk, CB8 7QB
Tel: 0845 371 0518
www.mr-fothergills.co.uk
Suppliers of a wide range of vegetables,
flowers and herbs

Nickys Nursery Ltd.
Fairfield Road, Broadstairs, Kent, CT10 2JU
Tel: 01843 600972
http://www.nickys-nursery.co.uk
A range of vegetable and herb seeds,
including some unusual varieties

The Organic Gardening Catalogue
Riverdene Business Park, Molesey Road,
Hersham, Surrey, KT12 4RG
Tel: 01932 253666
www.organiccatalogue.com
The official mail order catalogue of Garden
Organic, the organic association. Heritage
varieties available

The Real Seed Catalogue

Real Seeds, PO Box 18, Newport near
Fishguard, Pembrokeshire, SA65 0AA
Tel: 01239 821107
www.realseeds.co.uk
A particularly good source of unusual
Mediterranean cultivars, all trialled
by the owners for their suitability
to cooler climates

Seeds of Italy

D2 Phoenix Business Centre,
Rosslyn Crescent, Harrow, Middx, HA1 2SP
Tel: 0208 427 5020
www.seedsofitaly.com
A wide range of vegetable and herb seeds,
particularly Continental varieties

Simpsons Seeds

The Walled Garden Nursery,
Horningsham, Wiltshire, BA12 7NQ.
Tel: 01985 845004
www.simpsonsseeds.co.uk
Suppliers of vegetable seeds and seedlings,
specializing in hard-to-find and less well-
known varieties

Suffolk Herbs (Kings Seeds)

Monks Farm, Coggeshall Road,
Kelvedon, Essex, CO5 9PG
Tel: 01376 570000
www.kingsseeds.com
A good range of vegetable and herb seeds

Suttons Seeds

Woodview Road, Paignton, Devon, TQ4 7NG
Tel: 0844 9220606 (orders) 03334002899
(customer service)
http://www.suttons.co.uk
Suppliers of a wide range of vegetables,
flowers and herbs

Thompson & Morgan

Poplar Lane, Ipswich Suffolk, IP8 3BU
Tel: 0844 573 1818
www.thompson-morgan.com
Suppliers of a wide range
of vegetables, flowers and herbs

Unwins Seeds

Alconbury Hill, Huntingdon,
Cambs, PE28 4HY
Tel: 0844 573 8400
www.unwins.co.uk
Suppliers of a wide range of
vegetables, flowers and herbs

FRUIT SUPPLIERS:

Ken Muir

Honeypot Farm, Rectory Road,
Weeley Heath, Clacton-on-Sea,
Essex, CO16 9BJ
Tel: 01255 8301534
www.kenmuir.co.uk

Keepers Nursery

Gallants Court, East Farleigh,
Maidstone, Kent, ME15 0LE
Tel: 01622 726465
www.keepers-nursery.co.uk

Chris Bowers, Whispering Trees Nurseries

Wimbotsham, Norfolk, PE34 3QB
Tel: 01366 388752
www.chrisbowers.co.uk

Blackmoor Nurseries

Blackmoor, Nr Liss, Hampshire, GU33 6BS
Tel: 01420 477978
http://www.blackmoor.co.uk

Further reading

Grow Your Own Vegetables, by Joy Larkcom
(Frances Lincoln, 2002)

Organic Gardening, by Lawrence D. Hills
(Penguin, 1977)

RHS Pests and Diseases, by Pippa Greenwood and Andrew Halstead
(Dorling Kindersley, 2009)

RHS Fruit and Vegetable Gardening, by Michael Pollock
(Dorling Kindersley, 2002)

HDRA Encyclopedia of Organic Gardening, editor-in-chief Pauline Pears
(Dorling Kindersley, 2005)

The New Vegetable and Herb Expert, by D.G. Hessayon
(Expert Books, 2014)

The New Fruit Expert, by D.G. Hessayon
(Expert Books, 2015)

RHS Horticultural Show Handbook
(Royal Horticultural Society 2008)
A useful book if you get serious about showing your fruit and veg at local competitions

Visit the RHS online at www.rhs.org.uk, where you will find a wealth of information. The RHS also publish a list of fruit and veg plants with an RHS Award of Garden Merit which is updated at intervals. It can be found online and is useful for its listing and description of fruit and vegetable varieties recommended by the RHS. RHS membership, either as a gift or for yourself, is certainly a helpful investment. As well as free access to all four RHS gardens, you can get free gardening advice and the RHS monthly magazine, *The Garden*. This magazine is full of practical advice, ideas and inspiration, and every issue will contain something relevant to the allotment gardener.
Tel: 02031765820 for more information, or visit www.rhs.org.uk/join.

Acknowledgements

Shutterstock: 1000 Words 125; 360b 76b; a40757 103bl; Air Images 98t; Aleksandar Todorovic 4–5; Alexander Raths 52, 67br, 95, 128; Alexey Stiop 79b; Alison Hancock 15, 149, 161; Ami Parikh 130; Andrii Opanasenko 85b; angelakatharina 195t; AnikaNes 182t; Ariene Studio 81t; Arina P Habick 8; Arkady_S 120; audaxl 23, 24, 49t, 156; auremar 176; Aygul Bulte 13, 50; basel101658 105; Bastiaanstock 76t; Betty Shelton 173tr; bikeriderlondon 6, 38, 78, 175, 186; BildagenturZoonar GmbH 98br, 169b; blackeagleEMJ 81b; Bobkeenan Photography 104bl; bofotolux 140; BrankoG 195bl; Candus Camera 189b; Cat_arch_angel 153 (oriental leaves); ChameleonsEye 71b, 85t; chrisbrignell 86t; Claus Mikosch 199; Cora Mueller 17; Cornelia Pithart 103tr; Crepesoles 117; D Russell 36–37; D. Pimborough 82t; Dancing Fish 80t; Debu55y 83b; DementevaJulia 77t; Denis and Yulia Pogostins 141r; Destinyweddingstudio 78b; Diana Taliun 44, 47, 102tl, 182br; DibasUA 53; Dirk Ott 33; Dmitry Bruskov 198; dovgan 195br; Durden Images 126–127; DUSAN ZIDAR 115; Eag1eEyes 49b, 135; EdCorey 46; EQRoy 87b; Erni 173bl, br; Federico Rostagno 64; FotobyRoy 79t; Frank Gaertner 72b; Gary Smith 197; gashgeron 97; Gemenacom 114; Gregory Johnston 84b; Heike Rau 159; Hintau Aliaksei 57l; holwichaikawee 141l; Igor Borodin 86b; Ingrid Balabanova 124; Iryna Loginova 122br; Issarawat Tattong 104tl; itman__47 84t; Jeanie333 147bl; johnbraid 28, 29, 30, 31, 32, 35, 116l, 164; JRB67 72m; Julia Lototskaya 192; Kevin Day 136t, 139b; Kingarion 101br, 142–143; KPG_Payless 153 (broad beans); krungchingpixs 74m; Ksenia Ragozina 54; Lana Smirnova 153 (beetroot); LiAndStudio 57r; LianeM 100; Linda George 69b; Lori Martin 68b; lzf 102br; Mark Bridger 173tl; MarkMirror 169t; MNStudio 179, 181; Monika Pa 92; Nadezhda Shoshina 153 (broccoli, leeks, spring onions, new potatoes, garlic); Naffarts 51, 67bl; Nataliia Melnychuk 168; Nikolay Dimitrov – ecobo 70t; nld 153 (winter cabbage, spring cabbage, brussels sprouts, shallots, celeriac, carrots, dwarf French beans); oceanfishing 74b, 145; Olivier Le Queinec 171; Papik 69t; Paul Maguire 65; Paul Nicholas UK 42–43; Phil Syme 80b; phomphan 87t; photogal 22, 101tl; photoiconix 1, 104tr; photopixel 112; photowind 146br; Pi-Lens 83t; Pixavril 150; Pressmaster 104br; ptashka 153 (mange tout); pwrmc 147t, 191; Quang Ho tags used throughout with or without string; rawcaptured 72t; Richard Griffin 101tr; richsouthwales 136; Ruta Saulyte-Laurinaviciene 167; sanddebeautheil 88–89, 90; Sarah2 189t; Sergii Chepulskyi 96; Sever180 73b; Shelli Jensen 106; Simone Andress 158; siraphat 77b; Sponner 70b; stefansonn 182bl; Steve Buckley 75b; steveball 39, 139t; stevemart 20, 78t, 109; Svetlana Foote 69m; Swapan Photography 122bl; Swellphotography 102bl; Tatiana Davidova 153 (cauliflower); Tatiana Volgutova 71t; Tatiana Vorona 193; thieury 41; Tim Large 18; travelscout 73b; TwilightArtPictures 154; twins_nika 153 (runner beans); Ursa Studio 62, 103tl; Vlad Siaber 103br; Volodymyr Baleha 101bl; vvoe 172; wentus 116r; WollertzShuterstock 14; yuris 73t, 82b, 98bl, 102tr; Zigzag Mountain Art 68t; Zocchi Roberto 184; Zygotehaasnobrain 110–111.

Alamy: Jane Williams 201

GAP: 122t, 133; Dave Bevan 166; Elke Borkowski 56, 59; Gary Smith 163; Gillian van Meer 107; Jonathan Buckley 165; Ray Cox 27; Simon Colmer 136bl; Suzie Gibbons 10–11

Wikipedia: Sten Porse 151

Index

Page numbers in *italics* indicate a caption to an illustration. Page numbers in **bold** indicate a main entry.